BANGKOK *BABYL*

"Man needs escape as he needs food and deep sleep."

—W.H. Auden

Bill Gorton: "You're an expatriate. You've lost touch with the soil. Fake European standards have ruined you. You drink yourself to death. You become obsessed by sex. You spend all your time talking, not working. You are an expatriate, see? You hang around cafes."

Jake Barnes: "It sounds like a swell life."

—Ernest Hemingway
The Sun Also Rises

"Are you prepared to be free?"

—Jimi Hendrix

BANGKOK *BABYLON*

JERRY HOPKINS

TUTTLE PUBLISHING
Tokyo • Rutland, Vermont • Singapore

Published by Tuttle Publishing, an imprint of Periplus Editions (HK) Ltd., with editorial offices at 364 Innovation Drive, North Clarendon, Vermont 05759 USA.

ISBN 978-0-8048-4077-4

Distributed by:

North America, Latin America & Europe
Tuttle Publishing
364 Innovation Drive
North Clarendon, VT 05759-9436 U.S.A.
Tel: 1 (802) 773-8930; Fax: 1 (802) 773-6993
info@tuttlepublishing.com
www.tuttlepublishing.com

Japan
Tuttle Publishing
Yaekari Building, 3rd Floor
5-4-12 Osaki, Shinagawa-ku
Tokyo 141 0032
Tel: (81) 03 5437-0171; Fax: (81) 03 5437-0755
tuttle-sales@gol.com

Asia Pacific
Berkeley Books Pte. Ltd.
61 Tai Seng Avenue, #02-12
Singapore 534167
Tel: (65) 6280-1330; Fax: (65) 6280-6290
inquiries@periplus.com.sg
www.periplus.com

12 11 10 09
6 5 4 3 2
Printed in the United States of America

Contents

Tony Poe, an American soldier, was wounded on Iwo Jima and later trained the men who brought the Dalai Lama out of Tibet and led the Hmong army in Laos. Presumed by many to be the inspiration for Colonel Kurtz in *Apocalypse Now*...

Jack Shirley, one of Tony's CIA classmates and his closest pal in Laos, trained hilltribe men—who'd previously never even seen a wheel—how to fly. After the war, he bought shares in several Patpong bars and sat at the end of one of them until his liver shriveled up...

Patrick Gauvain, a diminutive British citizen born in Malaysia, was a photographer who achieved legendary status for his annual bar girl calendars and alcohol-fueled, pyrotechnic behavior. He was later arrested on pornography charges, helping his already successful advertising business...

Joe Maier, an American Catholic priest who founded Mercy Centre in Bangkok's largest and meanest slum some twenty-five years ago. The organization now includes more than thirty kindergartens, the city's oldest AIDS hospice, five shelters for street kids and a legal-aid attack team that represents a hundred kids every month...

Jeab was a dancer in a bar where she met Ron, a Scotsman who married her and built her a house in the rice paddy. She gambled, he drank and soon all hell broke loose. After he died, she returned to the bar and met Villy, a romantic bus driver, who took her to Denmark and married her...

Richard Lair, who fell in love with elephants at the age of four, became one of the world's two or three foremost authorities on the domesticated Asian elephant. He helped found Thailand's only school for *mahouts* (elephant trainers), and taught elephants how to paint and play musical instruments...

John Gray was called "Caveman" because he was the first to explore and then exploit the lagoons in the center of small islands in the Phang Na Sea. He subsequently won eco-tourism awards around the world, and went up against the "Birds' Nest Mafia," a fight he did not win...

Byron Bales, an American private investigator who worked for Western insurance companies, tracked down runaway men who faked their deaths back home, many of whom still make a beeline for Thailand. He wrote a novel based on a "composite" of his cases, published it in Thailand, then retired there...

George Cooper, an American lawyer in Phnom Penh, won compensation for thousands of poor farmers whose land was stolen by the government; sent a Cambodian officer to jail and put away a Khmer Rouge leader who ordered the killing of three backpackers. Somehow, he hasn't had a mysterious, fatal accident yet...

Bernard Trink is a simultaneously loved and loathed journalist who covered the *farang* bar scene for thirty years in Thailand's English-language press. Later reduced to covering happy-hour schedules, he was fired when he reached his 70s, and took his gossip to the internet...

Stirling Silliphant was an Academy Award-winning screenwriter who wrote *In the Heat of the Night*, *The Poseiden Adventure*, *Towering Inferno* and many of television's most popular series. He moved to Thailand to die, because he didn't want it to happen anywhere else...

Eric Rosser, a talented pianist from the U.S., taught music to the children of the Bangkok elite. Then he became the first pedophile on the FBI's Ten Most Wanted list. He jumped bail, had plastic surgery and was re-arrested when he returned to Thailand...

Mark Parr, a clown in a canadian traveling circus who became a computer programmer, met **Duncan Kilburn**, another programmer who helped found a rock band called the Psychedelic Furs. Together, they opened a trendy Hong Kong restaurant called the Globe, then made the mistake of moving it to Phnom Penh...

Richard Diran spent more than twenty years buying gems and looted temple antiquities from Cambodia and Burma. He eventually returned to his first love, painting, while his wife accumulated more than a hundred fighting cocks, along with fourteen dogs and a small zoo of wild animals...

David Jacobson, a New York fashion photographer, opened what became Saigon's most exalted and profitable watering hole, the Q Bar. After a six-year battle with the Vietnamese government, he was barred from re-entering the country, then opened an equally prosperous bar with the same name in Bangkok...

William Warren, the "Dean of Expat Writers" with more than forty books in print, is the final word on most things culturally and historically Thai. The "amateur" landscaper has designed gardens for some of the country's finest hotels and has taught on all seven faculties at Chulalongkorn University...

Harold Stephens, a marine who fought the Japanese in World War II and was imprisoned by the Chinese Communists, sailed the Pacific (befriending Marlon Brando), climbed mountains with Hillary, explored lost cities, crossed Afghanistan on a camel and drove a motorcycle across Australia. Then he wrote it all down...

So, You Want to Own a Bar in Bangkok? 154

Big Steve Watson and Small Steve Bird were barflys of differing physiognomy and dues-paying members of the Vietnam Helicopter Association. Then they decided to stop spending their money in Bangkok's bars and buy one....

Hero/Entrepreneur 161

John Everingham, an Australian photographer in wartime Laos, helped blow the whistle on Air America and its connection to the opium trade. He famously crossed the Mekong River to Thailand using SCUBA gear to rescue his Lao girlfriend, then went on to operate a successful publishing company...

Rock Star 169

Rick Montembault, an American rock musician, refused to stand in line to audition for a twenty-minute rock band showcase in Los Angeles. He took his songbook and voice to Southeast Asia, and now fronts what may be Thailand's only fulltime *farang* rock group...

Class Clown 177

Jim Eckardt was one of America's numerous Peace Corps volunteers who chose not to return home. He bought a motorcycle in Singapore and headed for London, stopped permanently in Thailand, acquired a Thai wife, then struggled to put four children through school as a writer and author...

Lonely Planeteer 185

Joe Cummings is the author of thirty-five travel books, including, for the past twenty years, the Lonely Planet guides to Thailand. A frustrated rock star who once lost the use of a hand, he now jams with bands in Chiang Mai, has a new Thai wife, and plans to become a Thai citizen...

John Quincannon, an American Vietnam vet, worked for the American program that found new homes in the U.S. for displaced Vietnamese. He later became an English instructor for Thai school children and businessmen, and will do anything to avoid going home again...

Jason Schoonover, a onetime Canadian disc jockey, was inspired by the National Geographic magazine to go on adventures and collect ethnographic artifacts for museums and private collectors. He created an alter ego and made him the hero of three novels: a character known for the hair on his chest and his conversations with his own penis...

Dennis Cooper, an American enterpreneur, made a ton of money working weekends at America's Renaissance Pleasure Faires. He took his cash to Thailand, where he spends eight months each year with his Thai wife, owns a house upcountry, an apartment and part ownership in a Bangkok bar...

Jerry Hopkins, an American writer, revealed many of his friends' secrets and now reveals some of his own. He credits a two-headed cow with setting him on his lifelong quest for the unusual and believes that the key to success often is no more than being in the right place at the right time, and having an insatiable curiosity...

Tales from the Next Barstool

Not so long ago a friend in the United States sent me a story from *Penthouse* magazine about a legal case that had intrigued an international audience from its first reporting in the world's press. It concerned the unusual life and death of Larry Hillblom, the "H" in DHL Worldwide Express, the world's largest courier delivery service, who left behind an estate of about $600 million when his private plane mysteriously plunged into the Pacific Ocean in 1995. There was nothing extraordinary about that; it was just another tragic airplane crash—in fact, it was Hillblom's third. But then there emerged, accompanied by lawyers, a group of young women from Southeast Asia who said their six children were his...and they wanted a piece of the pie.

Those who knew Hillblom merely grinned when they heard the claims. Founding a bank in Saipan, investing in Air Micronesia and Continental Airlines, starting a resort community in Guam, and spending $40 million to renovate a French colonial hotel in Vietnam wasn't all he did in his spare time. He was also known to frequent some of Southeast Asia's more colorful bars.

Inasmuch as Hillblom's body was never found—and his will lacked the standard clause disinheriting illegitimate heirs—the attorneys were given permission by the court to visit the deceased's Saipan home to search for something that could be used to conduct DNA tests in their effort to prove Hillblom was the father. By the time they arrived, however, even the drains of the showers had been cleaned of all hairs or skin fragments and all personal effects reportedly were destroyed. Further, when the wreckage of the plane was recovered, the control panel and pilot's seat (where blood might have been detected) were missing and Hillblom's relatives refused to surrender samples of their own blood. Meanwhile, four of the children were declared by *their* DNA tests to share a common father. Interesting, but it didn't link them to Hillblom.

Finally a break came when Hillblom's mother changed her mind about providing a blood sample after being told she'd been cut from her son's will. Of course, she wanted to be paid. Lawyers for the plaintiffs agreed to give the woman a million dollars out of the offsprings' share of the legacy if the DNA tests made their case. A second break—the deciding one—came when a girlfriend told investigators where the man's clothing and personal effects had been buried when the mansion was super-cleaned. (For pointing to a spot next to the tennis courts, she, too, was promised a million dollars.) Soon after tests were conducted on hairs from a brush, the court ruled that the founder and DHL'S sole owner—by the time of his death, he'd bought his two partners' shares—was indeed the father of four of the children, and each was awarded $90 million!

Accompanying the magazine story when it arrived in the mail from my pal was the note, "You can never tell who's sitting on the next bar stool."

This is certainly true in Bangkok, where I live. I doubt I ever shared drinks with Larry Hillblom, but I'll bet that we drank in some of the same bars, and in the ten years that I've made my home in Thailand, I've drunk with many of his peers—expatriates who are bolder, more imaginative or more curious, and more heroic or foolhardy or over-the-top than most—men imbued with an unchecked sense of adventure—or, at least a delight in the eccentric (on a slow day), the unexpected (on an average day) and no less than the incredible (on a good day). Adventurers of both the indoor and outdoor types. Intellectual and physical explorers who are purposeful to the point of stubbornness, adamant in their quest for knowledge and experience. And the hell with what other people may think.

Thailand also attracts the con-men, law-breakers, runaways and what back home might be called sexual deviants. It is a place where erratically enforced laws are written by men who may not intend to stick to them—who, if they get caught, know they'll do little or no time in jail because the fix is almost a political certainty or is, at worst, bargain-priced. So it is, too, for many foreigners who seek refuge here, in the same way that—not so many years ago—bank robbers and scam artists sought escape in the Bahamas and Latin America.

The phrase "wild, wild east" is a cliché, yet it is both reasonable and accurate when applied to what is, undeniably, one of the great, unruly and untamed cities in the world. Bangkok is Y-chromosome territory, a city where surprise is as ordinary as bad air and traffic jams and pretty, young women and rice; where accessibility and affordability accompany anything you want, even unleashed fantasy. Sex, drugs, counterfeit designer goods and software, smuggled gems, weapons, endangered species…Thailand is Southeast Asia's prime marketplace. It's not surprising that such an environment has appeal for some of what society deems the best and the worst. Missionaries and NGOs come to fix the "problem." Others come to roll around in it.

Once when I was sitting belly-up to the stage in a go-go joint in one of Bangkok's numerous testosterone districts, I struck up a conversation with the guy sitting next to me. He told me he worked for America's Orderly Departure Program, helping relocate Vietnamese to the post-war United States. He also played a role in breaking the story on *60 Minutes* about how the CIA secretly trained and air-dropped South Vietnamese spies to infiltrate Hanoi; every one was captured and tortured or executed, and my new friend was involved, a quarter of a century later, in helping their families get visas to the U.S., along with compensation.

Another time, the next bar stool (different bar) was occupied by an Oscar-winning screenwriter who told me he migrated to Bangkok because he couldn't think of a nicer place to die. I met two foreigners who came to find Thai wives, and two American bar owners (helicopter pilots left over from the Vietnam war) who introduced them to the same woman (both married her)...a feisty American Catholic priest who lived and waged war against poverty and the Thai establishment while living in the slums for thirty-five years...an Australian photographer who helped blow the whistle on Air America's involvement in the heroin trade, swam across the Mekong River with his Laotian sweetie on his back, then went on to run a successful publishing company...another photographer (British) who made a name for himself selling bar girl calendars and ran an advertising agency that told five-star hotels and international corporations how to succeed in business...an American man who taught elephants to paint and play musical instruments, then sold the paintings for $500 apiece on the National Geographic Channel and got international distribution for two CDs...a Canadian circus dwarf and an English rock musician with a common interest in computer programming who opened a restaurant together, and a Yank lawyer who put Khmer Rouge officers in jail, all residents of Phnom Penh who came to Bangkok to celebrate their victories...the U.S. Marine many people believe was the model for Marlon Brando's Colonel Kurtz in *Apocalypse Now*, and his best friend who stayed in Bangkok following the Vietnam war to become a "fixer" for Hollywood filmmakers (both were in the CIA)...the son of J. Edgar Hoover's secretary who taught English to Thai school children and businessmen...a bounty hunter who tracked down men who faked their deaths to collect million-dollar insurance policies...a gemologist who dealt in looted antiquities from Burma and Cambodia...and a high-society piano player at one of the world's most acclaimed hotels who became the first pedophile on the FBI's Ten Most Wanted list.

In Bangkok, as in few, if any, other places on earth, Larry Hillblom was just one of the guys, one of the legion who escaped from their past to recreate or find or lose themselves through travel. No less an authority on the subject than Somerset Maugham wrote, "It seemed to me that by a long journey to some far distant country I might renew myself...I journeyed to the Far East. Went looking for adventure and romance, and so I found them...but I found also something I had never expected. I found a new self."

The tales that follow may be out of the ordinary even in Bangkok, but they are not exceptional. One of the reasons I migrated to Thailand was because it had the most interesting expatriate community I'd encountered anywhere in the world. And for those considering going down the same path, it's important, obviously, to know who some of your new friends might be.

Some of the characters in this book wear white hats (if smudged). Some wear black ones. I don't pretend that they reflect the overall expat community—there are a disproportionate number of Americans and media types, no surprise given they were selected by an American writer—and business heads and NGOs are woefully under-represented. Still, they have much in common with the larger expat community. Nearly all are long-timers and most have become disaffiliated from their home countries, many to the point of feeling like an alien when they return for a visit. Usually, things back home have changed...and in every case the expat has altered his psychology, if not his chemistry. And almost always, apparently quite comfortably.

At the same time, in their adopted country they remain outside. No matter how fluent in the language and adept in hurdling the cultural barriers they may be, forever they will be foreigners, what in Thailand are called *farangs*. Yet, they are foreigners who can, as outsiders, reveal some of the secrets of Southeast Asia—a region long tangled in adventure and mystery (and bullshit)—that may be off the usual traveler's path, but may also be, in fact, never more distant than around the next corner or sitting slumped over a beer on the next bar stool.

Consider this collection of profiles a how-to book, and let the expats be your guides. If you want a new experience, or want to re-invent yourself, or want escape, even if for just a night, or merely want a vicarious thrill or two, then this is the way, follow me.

When in Bangkok, do what your mama told you never to do.

Talk to a stranger.

The Real Colonel Kurtz?

When I heard that the government had kicked him out of the country, that he was persona non grata in Thailand after making it his choice of residency for twenty years, I wondered: what could anyone do that might be considered so offensive in Thailand as to justify deportation? When it came to behavior, this was the Southeast Asian country whose motto was *mai pen rai*, which is Thai for *que sera sera*. So long as you didn't badmouth Buddhism or royalty, it was a country known for its rampant hedonism and illegality. Anything you wanted or wanted to do was likely okay with the authorities, usually at an affordable price.

Tony Poe arguably was one of the most colorful characters of his time and place, in Sumatra, Tibet and Laos from the 1950s through the 1970s, and Thailand in the years that followed. He was one of many survivors of America's "secret war" who decided not to go back to the United States when the Yanks packed it in and left what used to be called Indochine to the Communists. Hundreds of these ex-warriors stayed in Thailand, where they lived—and some still reside—many with their Asian wives and kids, operating businesses, and nursing livers as defeated as the armed forces with whom they fought.

I never knowingly drank with Tony, although I might have; I drank in some of the same bars with his friends. One of them was Jack Shirley, with whom Tony ran Operation Momentum, the secret U.S. program aimed at organizing the Lao hilltribesmen into an anti-Communist army, so that it would seem that the opposition to the Viet Cong was homegrown rather than comprised of U.S. forces, who had no legal right to be in Laos in any case.

Tony's grandparents immigrated to the United States from Prague in the 1880s, settling in Milwaukee, where grandfather Anton became a successful baker. Tony's father, John Poshepny, served thirty-five years in the Navy and while stationed in Guam, married a native of the island named Isabella. Tony was raised in California—born in Long Beach in 1924, attending high school in Santa Rosa—and at age nine was accidentally shot in the stomach by his brother. Soon after his eighteenth birthday, he enlisted in the Marines, served with a parachute battalion in the southwest Pacific and then was leader of a machine gun team that invaded Iwo Jima. On the fifteenth day of what was one of the bloodiest battles of the war, he was wounded in the leg, recovering in time to join the initial occupation force sent to a defeated Japan.

After the war, Tony went to college on the G.I. Bill, graduating in 1950 with a degree in English and history from San Jose State, where he was known for his prowess on the golf course. This improbable encounter with the straight world apparently had little effect and in 1951, he applied for a job with the FBI, whose recruiter referred him to the CIA training school at Camp Peary, Virginia. He graduated in one of the organization's first classes. Shirley was one of his classmates and both were sent to Asia: Jack to help organize the Thai Border Police, Tony to work with members of an animist-Christian sect that had fled North Korea and were being trained to be sent back as saboteurs.

When the Korean "police action" ended, he was sent to Thailand for five years and then assigned to a CIA team involved in an attempt to overthrow the Sukarno regime in Indonesia—an effort that included an arduous 150-kilometer trek through jungle and over mountains for emergency evacuation by submarine. That was followed by an assignment to train the Khamba tribesmen who in 1958 smuggled the young Dalai Lama out of Tibet.

Thus, Poe already had a reputation as the Ultimate Drill Instructor by the time he arrived, in Laos in 1961. The French, who colonized what is now Vietnam, Laos and Cambodia, had been defeated by the Vietminh in 1954, and less than three months later, a conference in Geneva cut Vietnam in half. The Americans, who had paid for much of the French war's final years, moved in, believing that if the puppet South Vietnamese government fell in Ho Chi Minh's drive to reunite his country, the rest of Southeast Asia would tumble like dominoes. This theory was used to justify the U.S. war in Vietnam, a six-year-long conflict that killed nearly fifty nine thousand American troops and an estimated million Vietnamese. Poe was one of the men sent in to stop Uncle Ho's advance, specifically to protect the Laos border with Vietnam and inhibit the Vietcong's use of Laos territory that bordered North and South Vietnam along what was called the Ho Chi Minh Trail.

Here, along with the Thai border police (working with Shirley again), he helped train Hmong tribesmen who at a peak strength of thirty thousand were the only effective Lao army, delivering to his agency bosses a fighting force that gave the Commies fits, but came with "liabilities," some of the most damaging to Tony himself. This also was where, and when, the Legend of Tony Poe began, along with his heavy drinking.

He liked telling a story about going to the Chinese border for a week-long assault on a Vietcong-held Laotian village where some of his soldiers had family, using that as a carrot to get his attack force highly motivated. When the U.S. ambassador in Vientiane heard about the plan, he blew his stack, worried that the incident might bring China into the war. Tony's status was not improved some time later when, drunk, he came to a meeting at the ambassador's office with a rifle in one hand, a machete in the other. Still another time, when someone was sent to rein him in, Tony reportedly flew the guy across the Chinese border and threatened to land and leave him there. Another version of the story said he threatened to throw the guy out of the moving chopper.

In 1965, he was living in a remote village in northern Laos, subsisting on government rations and whatever was locally available, isolated by the lack of electricity, roads and phones. The enemy approached as he sat outside his grass-roofed hut drinking scotch. He picked up an M-1 carbine and shot seventeen of them, according to friends' accounts, while taking a bullet in the pelvis that exited through his stomach. Using his rifle as a crutch, he then limped to a friendly camp some miles away, where he insisted a helicopter go back for his wounded troops before taking him to safety; if you don't take care of your troops, he said, you can't expect them to take your orders. Fearing his continued illegal presence in Laos would be discovered by the press if taken to a hospital in Vientiane, he was airlifted back to Thailand, the official story being that he was a U.S. Air Force crewman shot down in "neutral" Laos.

The tales piled up like apocrypha and it was when he offered his troops a one-dollar bounty for every pair of Commie ears turned in, then strung them from the eaves of his house, carried them around in paper bags to shock new arrivals in-country, and stapled them to his official reports when his body count was questioned, that his reputation as a barberous sonofabitch was set. The way Tony told the story, he stopped the practice when he encountered a twelve-year-old boy with no ears and was told his daddy cut them off for the reward. After that, Tony paid $10 for heads, providing they came with a Vietcong cap. When asked if it were true that he dropped those heads onto enemy encampments, he said he'd only done it twice, once to deliver a message to a hostile village headman who'd taken a shot at his plane.

There was another time, a friend swears, that as Tony was conversing in a Bangkok bar, beneath the table he was silently strangling a cat. Hospitalized in the same city with wounds from a "Bouncing Betty"—a mine that springs up when stepped on, exploding at chest-height—friends supposedly sent him a bottle of vodka with a prostitute and, they insist, he was expelled from the hospital despite the fact that his playtime with the hooker had ripped open several stitches. He also lost two fingers when trying to defuse a booby-trap, leaving him with a claw that he used, when drunk, to great dramatic effect.

At the same time, he was a true friend of the hilltribe people, who came to accept him as probably few if any other foreigners before had ever been embraced. He learned enough of several dialects to converse, he lived with them for years at a time, he got knee-walking drunk with them on home brew that sometimes was flavored with a large centipede, he never asked them to do anything he wouldn't do himself, and, defying CIA policy, he married the niece of Touby Ly Foung, the Hmong chief, with whom he had two daughters.

The head of the CIA at that time, Bill Lair, said, "He was an actor who loved to play a part but then he forgot who he really was. I put that man in the jungle, in charge of primitive people, and gave him absolute power over them. They watched him perform magic, call in air strikes and saw rice and guns fall from the sky. They believed he was some sort of god."

Consequently, it was no surprise when, years later, some in the media, including CBS TV in the U.S. and England's BBC, said the Marlon Brando figure in *Apocalypse Now* was inspired by Poe. Tony laughed and the film's director and co-writer, Francis Ford Coppola, reasonably denied the comparison, but certainly they had a lot in common, right down to the devoted hilltribe follow-ing and the severed enemy heads. When the original Kurtz was executed in the Joseph Conrad novel that inspired the film's script, *Heart of Darkness*, his final words were the same ones that ended the movie: "The horror, the horror..." That seemed to fit Tony Poe, too.

In the end, Tony was an embarrassment to his employers, a man who not only broke all the rules—some with permission, after all—but also was impossible to control and, eventually, consumed two bottles of whisky a day. ("I drank before I went out to kill," he said. "There's nothing wrong with that.") Although he fought in the cause of anti-communism for a decade in Southeast Asia, when he returned to the United States for a CIA retirement cere-mony, he was perfunctorily thanked and told to get the hell out of town. One of the pilots recalled, "I drove him out to the National Airport afterward, accompanied by some Agency people who seemed to want to make sure he got on the plane, and it was as if they couldn't get him out of D.C. fast enough."

Tony shrugged philosophically when asked to react, quoting Rudyard Kipling: "It's Tommy this, an' Tommy that, and 'chuck him out, the brute!' But it's 'Savior of the country' when the guns begin to shoot..."

By the time the U.S. cut Tony loose in 1975—after he replaced Jack Shirley as head of training for four years in Thailand—he had more than thirty years in, enough for a military pension sufficient to live on comfortably in Thailand, so he settled with his wife in Udon Thani, the province where America had had one of its largest air bases and from which his old friend Bill Lair and the CIA had directed many of its wartime shenanigans. There were hundreds of disgruntled vets living there in raucous camaraderie, and Tony devoted his life to his family and raised sugar and cas-sava (tapioca). His demeanor was still subservient and polite when sober, calling everyone "sir," as many career non-commissioned officers tend to do in civilian life, his drunken bar episodes cut back slightly by 1980 when he was diagnosed with diabetes.

His binges continued, nonetheless, and turned into violent anti-American rants—many of the stay-behind vets felt abandoned, even betrayed by the U.S. withdrawal from the war—and eventually Tony's swaggering drunks and bar "disagreements"—his .45 often strapped to his waist—eroded the patience of even the most good-natured Thais. He was tricked into going to Bangkok, where his passport was taken away and he was put on a plane for the U.S. It was made clear that he would not be welcome back.

At first, he settled with his family in Fresno, a city in California's agricultural belt, then home to thirty thousand relocated Hmong who still regarded him as a sort of demi-god, and then moved to a small house in San Francisco. More than a dozen medals hung in neat rows in a glass case in his home, including six purple hearts, but when an American magazine ran a story called "Meet the CIA's Greatest Killer," the photographs taken by the magazine showed him drinking an ice cream soda, blowing soap bubbles and pulling a grandchild's wagon full of toys, as if he were some sort of over-the-hill, pussycat with a killer tomcat's now romanticized and forgiven past. His social calendar was highlighted by weddings and other special occasions held by his Hmong friends who lived in the Bay Area. He called them "my people." They called him "father."

A few years ago in a California court, he fought a deportation order for one of the men who'd served with him in Laos, who was convicted of opium possession. Tony testified for the man, saying his contribution to America's anti-communism crusade outweighed his opium charge. The judge agreed.

Tony Poe died in July, 2003, at the age of seventy-eight, following surgery to remove his second leg, both lost to the ravages of diabetes. His death followed by only three months that of his former CIA classmate Jack Shirley. Over the years, they had become adversaries, known for their loud arguments and brutal fistfights, and when Tony's demise was flashed by email and telephone to the Vietnam/Lao spook survivors, one of them said, "Wherever they are, I'm sure they have each other in a headlock."

Spy, Fixer, Raconteur

The man's shape was formed by years of beer consumed sitting on the stool at the end the Madrid Bar in Patpong. When other regulars entered, they said, "How are you?" "Not bad," he replied, "for a man with no liver." The *Bangkok Post* was opened on the bar in front of him, one hand held a mug of Klausthaler, the non-alcoholic beer that his doctor prescribed, the other was fitted to a bargirl's left buttock. It was one of the smallest bars in what's usually called Bangkok's "most notorious red-light district," and it was almost noon.

An old friend slid onto the stool next to Jack Shirley, the old CIA spook who owned a piece of the place and a legend left over from the "secret" war in Laos. Jack folded the paper, gave the girl a final squeeze, and started to reminisce. The stories fell onto the bar top like handguns dumped from a sack.

There was the time he was drinking in another bar when a former Russian KGB agent named Boris challenged him to a pushup contest. The war in Laos was long over and Jack looked a bit of a mess, but he hit the floor and pumped a hundred. As soon as the Russian executed his 101st, Jack kicked him in the head hard enough to knock him senseless. A week later, when Jack was drinking there again, Boris joined him, still six colors of the rainbow from the kick. Boris greeted Jack with a grin and merely said, "You got me that time."

This was Jack Shirley at peace. At war for the CIA and when he was farmed out to the U.S. Drug Enforcement Agency, he didn't kick, he killed. By his own admission, he was a hit man, a "journeyman killer" who claimed to have "zapped" an even dozen bad guys for his government. There was the time he was sent to Hong Kong Island to make a heroin buy, and on the way out of the building, he "accidentally" bumped into another spook, transferring the smack so that when, as expected, he stepped off the Star Ferry onto Kowloon and was jumped by the cops, he was clean and had to be let go. The dealer had set him up and bribed the cops so he'd get his heroin back.

A couple of months later, Jack set up another deal with the same dealer, this time a "big sell" that was to take place in a luxury house in Hua Hin, two hours south of Bangkok. His old friend Tony Poe was inside the house and Jack was outside in the bushes. A car pulled up with two occupants, the dealer and his driver/bodyguard. The dealer went inside. Jack strolled up to the car and zapped the driver, but before he could get to the house, he heard a gunshot. As Jack burst in, there was Tony holding a pistol and grinning over the dealer's corpse. Jack told friends at the bar he was pissed; he'd wanted to slap the dealer around first, have a go at him for trying to get him busted in Hong Kong.

Then there was the time in Laos when he was chased by the North Vietnamese for five days around torturous mountain trails. He and Tony and some other top CIA para-military officers had divided the country into five parts in 1961, back when *any* foreign presence there was prohibited by the Geneva Accords that followed Vietnam's defeat of the French. They then organized the Hmong hilltribe into an army to fight the Communist Laotian

Pathet Lao and the North Vietnamese Army, who crossed the border into Laos at the head of the Ho Chi Minh Trail, then being used to funnel troops and supplies from North to South Vietnam. Jack got the village headmen together and told them he'd supply all the guns and ammo they needed. They wanted to know how much it would cost. He said nothing and they laughed. Jack made a call on his walkie-talkie and the next day crates of weaponry fell from the sky. That's when the Hmong pledged their allegiance, and the North Vietnamese started chasing him.

Another time, he and Tony identified an avowed neutral Lao general who was really working for the communists, so they set up his assassination. They knew which whorehouse he frequented and bribed his favorite girl to give them the time and room number for his next visit. When the general entered the brothel, Jack and Tony flipped a coin to see who got to zap the guy. Tony won. After screwing in silencers, Tony went through the front door, Jack in the back, and Jack reached the girl's door first. He waited for Tony, but the designated killer was delayed for some reason. Worse, the general was a known premature ejaculator and Jack could tell from the girl's voice—remember that she was being paid by Jack and Tony—that the general was getting dressed. Jack couldn't wait any longer: he kicked in the door and did his patriotic duty.

He said he got his first taste for killing as a boy growing up in Maine, where he "bagged" more deer than he could remember. Later, as one of the CIA's earliest recruits, he trained in the same class with Poe at Camp Peary, before the present offices in Langley, Virginia, were built. One of Jack's first assignments was to accompany small airplanes that the U.S. government gave to the Thai government to set up what became the Border Patrol Police. Jack stayed on to train the flying cops—becoming the first and perhaps only foreigner to wear a Thai police uniform—and was given the rank of captain. He also inaugurated the police parachute training school at Hua Hin—one of the reasons so many cops on the street today wear parachute badges on their shirts—and was instrumental in setting up camps in the North and Northeast along the Laos border which became crucial during the war in Laos and for drug interdiction.

In 1970, Jack returned to the States for an official "retirement" and Tony took his place; once merely competitive partners, by now they were virulent antagonists, rarely speaking at fewer than eighty decibels, equal to a gunshot. As the war wound down—a truce was signed in Paris in 1973 and the communists took Laos along with Vietnam two years later—Jack returned to Thailand as a "civilian" police advisor, settling in Hua Hin and running the paratroop school. He also began investing, along with other ex-CIA spooks, in the new bars that were opening to accommodate the "sex tourists" that were replacing the GIs on R&R.

For many years, Jack and his fellow spies and onetime professional warriors hung their beer bellies on the bar at Lucy's Tiger Den, a joint on Suriwong Road that had a large banner that said it was the designated watering hole for members of China Post One of the American Legion Operating in Exile Out of Shanghai, a holdover from General Chennault's Flying Tigers of World War II. When Lucy's closed, Jack moved to the Madrid Bar around the corner in Patpong. This is where we met, in 1995, when I fortuitously sat next to him. When we introduced ourselves and I said I was a writer and he asked what I was working on and I said a story about how Hollywood movies got made in Thailand, he said, "So that's why you're here?"

"No," I said, "I came for the bean soup and corn bread."

"You don't know who I am?" I said I did not and he laughed so hard he knocked over his beer. (This was in the pre-Klausthaler days when he drank Singha.) For the next two hours, he talked, skipping over the entire war—and the stories I'd hear later—to tell me how he earned thousands of dollars from Hollywood producers and never left his stool at the Madrid, using a cell phone to call his old cop friends, many of whom were now generals, to get permission to bend if not totally ignore the law in the interest of getting the movies made.

There was the time, he said, when Jean-Claude Van Damme wanted to blow up and sink a boat in the Chao Phrya River. That was a tricky one, he said, because he had to get approval from the cops on both sides of the river and get the maritime police to stop traffic on the river itself. After some special "fees" were paid, the boat was exploded and sunk. Another time, Oliver Stone wanted to shut down traffic on a main thoroughfare during rush hour. Occasionally, someone else needed a bar- or drug-related infraction overlooked.

Jack got his start as a "fixer" in 1977, when a Hollywood producer named Bob Rosen hired him to find locations and "grease the reels" for a Steve McQueen film. The story was based on a real one dating to World War II, when America's famed Flying Tigers, were being out-flown and out-gunned by Japan's newest contribution to aerial warfare, the Zero; McQueen and his Burmese sidekick (to be played by Charles Bronson) were to steal one of the enemy planes. John Frankenheimer was to direct.

The Deerhunter had been filmed in Thailand recently and the producers had been ripped off. Bob says now that it was because the film company didn't have anyone working on the inside. Jack took Bob to the Laos border, considered a prime site for filming, where he met top officers of the Border Patrol Police, who said they'd heard McQueen was fat, a side effect to cancer treatment that Bob didn't know anything about. Jack then took Frankenheimer to meet the prime minister, who gave the director permission to use the former U.S. air base in U-tapao, from which much of the bombing of Vietnam had been staged. Then McQueen revealed that he did have cancer and the part was offered to Clint Eastwood, who liked the script but didn't want to go to Thailand, so the movie was never made.

Impressed by Jack's access that went all the way up to the prime minister's office, Rosen returned to Hollywood and when he signed on to produce *Prophesy*, a horror movie, and he needed a chief of security, he invited Jack "to come and do something stupid." His job: keep anyone outside the camera crew from seeing the monster.

Bob called Jack again when he made *The Island*, Peter Benchley's follow-up to *Jaws*. This film, which was shot in Antigua, told the story of a band of modern pirates—the descendants of real pirates from three-hundred years before—who preyed on yachts. Centuries of inbreeding had resulted in a band of "freaks," so only the truly deranged and handicapped were cast. Jack's job was to keep them in line.

Ironically, he also was charged with keeping them sober. By then, Jack was methodically drinking himself to death. Rosen said he finally talked Jack into coming to the States to dry out. For three months, Jack lived with the Rosen family in Seattle, experiencing what Bob called an "amazing" recovery.

Back in Bangkok, he met a young Thai girl named Pen—in time, he would marry her—and for a while he dutifully drank the Klausthaler he had learned to hate. In time, he returned to the real thing and Pen accompanied him back to Seattle to dry out again. "His liver was pretty shot," Bob Rosen said, "but, again, when he stopped drinking, he got better." Bob said he also tried at this time to get Jack to make peace with Tony Poe, but when he called Tony in San Francisco, it wasn't long before they were threatening to kill one another.

Rosen was so entranced by Jack, he hired a screenwriter to write a treatment for a film based on his life. The way Bob tells the story, John Frankenheimer showed some interest for a while and so did novelist Joseph Heller, but at the time the project was presented, the CIA was "all short haircuts and James Bond, and to do Jack's story right, it had to be about a guy who drank too much and fucked up. In other words, a human." Other friends say Jack didn't like the treatment because Tony Poe played a role in the story that diminished his.

Unlike Tony—whose alcohol-fueled violence eventually led the Thai government to deport him (in 1991)—Jack was an amiable drunk. He enjoyed meeting new people, laughed a lot, and always deferred to anyone of superior rank or standing. When William Colby, the former head of the CIA, was in Bangkok and address-ed the Foreign Correspondents Club, one of Jack's friends— a former university professor—tore into Colby verbally, attacking some of his tactics and policies. Next day, when the friend told Jack what he'd done, Jack was aghast, accusing his friend of a breach of authority and propriety.

For the media, however, he held only the highest disdain, blaming them for "losing the war at home" and for calling America's efforts in Laos a failure. "Tell me," Jack asked, "how was a handful of CIA with a bunch of Air America pilots going to win against the goddamned Vietnamese army? We weren't the U.S. Army! We were a supportive side action to the main war. We kept tens of thousands of Vietnamese soldiers tied down in Laos, damaging the enemy's effectiveness in South Vietnam. We cut into their movement of supplies down the Ho Chi Minh Trail and we kept the commies from moving into Thailand. We never lost Laos by a military action. It was signed away by treaty after the fall of Vietnam!"

That more bombs were dropped on Laos than on Nazi Germany, and that the CIA left behind a country full of bomb craters, amputees on crutches and antipersonnel bomblets that still kill hundreds every year, was beside the point. Jack believed the cause was just. His hands were untainted, his conscience clear.

"Some people don't realize the CIA was created to do the things the country couldn't do out in the open. Absolutely nothing we did was legal," he said. "I don't feel bad or any remorse whatsoever about zapping those guys. It didn't feel any different than shooting all those deer."

As the drinking continued, in 2002, Pen thought a move two hours away to Pattaya might help, by distancing him from his drinking buddies. It didn't even slow him down. Nor did a big sign that was hung in his favorite bar: "JACK 1, COMMUNISTS 0... SINGHA 1, JACK 0." Now he visited Bangkok only to see his doctor. Yet, his health continued to fail. He started talking about cremation, calling it "my barbecue."

The "barbecue" was held in Pattaya in April 2003. Nearly two hundred friends came to the send-off, including an emissary sent by Thailand's royal family, bearing the flame to light Jack's pyre in gratitude for his work on Thailand's behalf. He was seventy-six.

Jumbo Shrimp

I started hearing stories about a man called Patrick "Shrimp" Gauvain long before I moved to Thailand, and I'm still hearing them. Complete strangers seem anxious to pass along the lurid anecdotes in the fashion, I suppose, that tall tales were once spun about figures in ancient epics and myths.

Had I heard, I was asked in near worshipful tones, about the time that Shrimp paid the bar fine for fifty bar girls and had them delivered in a fleet of taxis to a friend as a birthday present? Or the time he took a dozen home for himself?

Then there was the time that he somehow dipped his penis into Kurt Waldheim's drink when the German diplomat wasn't looking. Or so I was told, but years later he corrected me, saying "actually, it was dipped into the soup of the lady sitting next to me at dinner, the Korean wife of a well-respected English expat who inquiringly asked, 'Is this the inter-course?'"

Another time, someone said, Shrimp saw a woman without arms selling flower garlands at an intersection, bought all of her flowers and took her home.

And, a friend asked, did I know that Shrimp kept a John Wayne outfit at the Eden Club, a big hat and chaps worn without jeans or knickers beneath?

Somebody else said he'd been detained once for "mopeny." What's that? I asked. My informant said he wasn't sure, but didn't it sound like something Shrimp would do?

More realistically, had I heard about the time he was driving a hundred kilometers an hour down a highway when a cop by the side of the road waved at him? Shrimp glanced at his watch, saw that it was nearly noon and knowing that the police were poorly paid, he figured the guy was just looking for money to buy lunch. He asked a friend who was in the car with him to give him all his small bills, knowing that the first cop would call another ahead of them. Sure enough, the second officer stood in the middle of the highway, his gun pointed at Shrimp's car. Whereupon, Shrimp held a fist full of money out the window as he approached and, as the cop deftly stepped aside, Shrimp released the packet of bills into his car's backwash.

As the stories piled up, my only tangible contact with the contemporary Dionysus was through the purchase of the wall calendars he sold in the bars: lubricious tributes to local beauty that proved to our buddies back home that we weren't lying about Bangkok's extraordinary citizenry. I finally met Shrimp and if we didn't exactly become bosom buddies, we ran in the same circles and became friends.

Still, it was years before I asked him about these tales and his story poured forth as if I'd opened a zipper on a rain cloud. "I was born in Malaysia," he said. "My father was Henry Gauvain. He was the king's physician and he also took care of the general who was in charge of the British Army in Malaysia. He was sort of a naughty fellow. He liked the booze and he liked the women. He got court martialed for crashing the general's car and generally misbehaving, and was transferred to some comfortable diplomatic position somewhere.

"My mother divorced him. She was having a few flings with the young studs in Penang anyway, so we all went back to the U.K. where she married 'the Milkman,' one of the gentlemen who ran United Dairies. Not long after that, she divorced him and married another person, also military. She liked men in uniforms." The memory inspires a smirk and Shrimp adds, "I kind of like girls in uniforms, too."

All this, Shrimp says, occurred before he was eight years old. Psychologists generally agree that when it comes to a person's future behavior and personality, it's the first seven years that count most. That, and genes. Clearly, he was a chip off his DNA.

His education was in English boarding schools, where an unusually tall roommate called him "Shrimp" and he said the nickname stuck. I interrupted his recitation at this point and asked how tall he was. He swore that he didn't know. Oh, come on, I said, every male knows two of his measurements and height is one of them. No, he insisted, he did not. I did not ask about length.

Upon graduation from university, he said, he joined a design studio in London, then accompanied a friend to Japan, traveling across the Soviet Union on the Trans-Siberian Express. In the half dozen years that followed, he photographed rock bands and taught English in Tokyo, and spent three months driving back to England with a Japanese girlfriend. In Afghanistan, he jokingly offered her in exchange for a coat he liked, but the merchant took him seriously and chased them around Kabul for half a day.

Back in Britain, he painted for a time in Wales, then returned to Japan to work for *Yomiuri Shimbun*, a newspaper that sent him undercover to report on the left-wing student movement. This got him arrested and he fled to Korea, returned again, then was sent to Saigon in 1968, just as the Tet offensive began, rockets coming into the airport at the very moment his plane landed. That was enough war for him, he said, and he caught the next flight out and spent several months in Cambodia, resigning from the newspaper just ahead of being fired, then crossed by train into Thailand, deciding, finally, to put down roots.

At the time, he had a full head of dark, wavy hair, worn to below his shoulders, and a Beefeater's mustache that curled up at the ends, a style that attracted the Military Police when he visited the Petchburi Road bars frequented by GIs on R&R from the war in Vietnam; they figured he was a deserter. With a camera and three lenses and a portfolio, he made the rounds of the international advertising agencies and in 1976 began Shrimp Studios, a commercial photo business that grew into a full-service ad agency with clients that included the Peninsula Group [hotels], Shangri-La Hotels, KLM Royal Dutch Airlines, Volvo and Jim Thompson Silk.

"These were euphoric years," he recalls, "spent in the floating brothels of Saen Saep Canal and along the *sois* of forbidden Bangkok, searching out young maidens, capturing their innocence."

In the early 1980s he was shooting covers and centerfolds for a Thai magazine whose name translated *Life Must Go On*. When a friend saw the extent of his library of such "innocents," he suggested Shrimp produce a calendar. Together, they printed a thousand copies and sold them all in a couple of weeks, to customers and bar owners in Patpong, a "red light" district that had replaced Petchburi Road as a destination for Thailand's growing sex industry. The next year, he did it again and from 1985 to 1989, he says, "It absolutely went ballistic. We were printing fifteen thousand calendars a year!"

His photographic subjects were of a type. Invariably, they were young and lithe, and usually they had perky, upturned breasts. (Once when I was in a bar with Shrimp, and when a dancer with large breasts appeared, he called her a "cow.") Still, most in the calendars and books showed none of the "innocence" that some might expect with youth.

A book of his photographs was published in Singapore and Shrimp disliked the way it was done, so he bought back the rights and in 1989 produced another himself, simply titled *Thai Girls*. Roman Polanski agreed to write the foreword, but his lawyer said no, because of recent pedophilia charges filed in Los Angeles (that would keep him out of the United States for what now appears to be forever), so it was written by Emmanuelle Arsan, star of the film that took her first name as its title and helped put Thailand on the erotic map, internationally. Not surprisingly, Shrimp was the film's still photographer.

A pre-launch party was held in London in a Thai restaurant in Knightsbridge. Shrimp flew four of the young "innocents" from the book in for the occasion and some Thais "whose names shall not be mentioned showed up. These guys chased the girls and I had them thrown out. These guys were quite influential and back in Bangkok they went to the Tourism Authority of Thailand and the Tourist Police, who came to my office and arrested me, just as I was on my way to see a client in Amsterdam." Shrimp's picture was on the front page of the *Bangkok Post* the next day under the headline, "Shrimp Flees Bangkok." Following numerous legal delays, he was fined the equivalent of $28.

Did the publicity hurt his business, now that he was labeled a "pornographer"? I asked. No, Shrimp said, it helped.

At the same time, Shrimp got involved with some Hong Kong businessmen who wanted to use his name to create a major enterprise like Playboy, calling it The Shrimp Club. Members were to be offered discounts at more than two hundred hotels, nightclubs, pubs and bars and, more enticing, there were to be invitations to auditions ("Help select the lucky ladies"), photoshoots ("Get to 'work' with Shrimp on location") and cruises ("Fun on the water with Shrimp models"). A catalog further offered lapel pins, desk and wallet calendars, wristwatches, key rings, neckties, post cards and upon joining, a complimentary bottle of something called

Contact 18, "the Pheromone Fragrance that makes every man irresistible to women." In 1995, after "realizing this was not a beneficial relationship," Shrimp took everything back.

The unsold shrimp pins were given to guests two years later when Shrimp celebrated his fiftieth birthday with a black-tie party in the grand ballroom of a posh Bangkok hotel. I bought my first tux for the event. Besides the feast that humbled any five-star Sunday buffet, he hired the city's top transvestite cabaret to entertain and had Thailand's top of the pops, Tata Young, sing happy birthday to him.

By the turn of the century, I thought Shrimp might have let his boozy exploits get a touch out of hand. At a dinner I attended at the Oriental Hotel, one of the other guests was a Hong Kong businessman Shrimp said he was courting as a client. By ten o'clock, time for the piano player to go home, Shrimp was standing on the table, yelling at him to play on. The prospective client quietly picked up the tab when Shrimp wasn't looking and sneaked out. Another time, I joined Shrimp for lunch and he was legless before the final course. I decided then that he might be a before-lunch friend.

Another couple of years passed. To my surprise, he'd finally married Mayuree, the Thai woman he'd always rather dispassionately introduced as "the mother of my children," who were then seven and nine. His business, in the interim, not only survived but blossomed, and by 2003 he had several "divisions" with a payroll of thirty and a client list that now included companies such as Nestle, Coca Cola, Holiday Inn, JW Marriott, the Peninsula and Oriental Hotels, Hilton and Playboy.

"One of the divisions is design development, taking care of the look, the design, style and manner of the company. It's brand engineering, really. You engineer the identity of their brand and put that brand out. Another is the photography for the advertising. Everything is interrelated. I also have a multi-media division for web site development, CD ROM, all the high-end computer tech aspects. Another division is signage systems. We design, manufacture, install and export signs for anything from a small restaurant to enormous commercial complexes. The last piece of business is outsourcing. We have a creative factory of computer artists, all Thais. Every morning we get ad briefs downloaded from the U.S. and in the evening we send the finished ads back, up to two hundred a day. For catalogs, magazines, phone directories."

Shrimp and I were having a "sober" lunch. (I drank two beers and he had a bloody Mary and a single glass of red wine) when he said this. "Sounds like a story of rehabilitation to me," I said.

Shrimp laughed and said, "Disgusting, isn't it?"

Yet another year passed, as I put this book aside for another project. When again we made plans to meet for a meal, I told him I wanted to confirm or have denied some of the wilder stories I'd heard, as well as get some more from him.

"You expect me to remember?" he said. He suggested a close friend come along to jog his memory. I agreed and learned that some of the stories were true and some probably were not, never mind which; what difference did it make? Does anyone really want to be told that Marco Polo didn't go to China or that Columbus didn't discover America?

The Italian meal was consumed, the wine bottle was empty, and another day was done. "So," I said, "how tall are you?" Again, he said he swore that he didn't know. Then he smiled, his now small mustache bristling beneath a bald head, and said in a whisper, "Five feet, five-and-a-half inches." It was as if he'd revealed his most sordid secret. Was I satisfied?

"Final question," I said. "Do you miss the calendars?"

"I'd be fool if I said I didn't."

He said that earlier in the year he'd produced six softcore videos for *Playboy* and was negotiating to shoot another six, under the title *Asian Angels*. He said he was also talking about shooting calendars for *Playboy*. I recalled an earlier assignment from Playboy that hadn't worked out when they refused to run his pictures because the models were too "dark."

"That was when they wanted the girl-next-door look," Shrimp explained. "Times have changed. Now my tastes are more acceptable."

Urban Guerilla Priest

Father Joe Maier took a seat at the table across from me, and as I ordered two mugs of Heineken draft, he took a call on his cell phone. It was January 2, 2000, the start of the new millennium, and we'd met to celebrate numerous past failures and occasional victories and a future of more of the same. A moment later, he ended his call, abruptly stood, and said, "There's been a gas leak at the ice house. You want to come along?"

We ran to his car, and as he sped through the Bangkok night, driving as I'd never seen him drive before, he explained that the place that produced ice for many of Bangkok's drinks was near his AIDS hospice and two of his shelters for street kids.

"Tell me what you know about freon," he said.

"I don't know much. What I remember from physics class is that it's an odorless, colorless gas that has no effect on humans, but according to more recent studies, it screws up the ozone layer. Why?"

He said that was what he was told was leaking into his neighborhood, the Klong Toey slum, the largest of some 1200 urban areas that were officially designated as slums in Bangkok. About a year earlier, Joe said, there'd been a fire in the ice house and it should've been shut down permanently, but the woman who owned it paid a visit to a local politician who paid a visit to the cops and nothing was done. That's the way troubles were handled in Bangkok.

We were still speeding through the streets, squealing as we hit the corners, bouncing into and out of pot holes. I laughed.

"What's so funny?"

"I had a thought. You know those movies where the cop's driving an unmarked car when he gets a call and he reaches out the window and puts one of those flashing lights on the roof? Where the light is stuck to the roof by a magnet and is plugged into the cigarette lighter? I just had an image of you doing that, except you have a flashing crucifix."

He laughed as we slid around another corner and the rest of the way to the ice house we argued about what kind of noise should be coming out of the car when the crucifix was in place. We agreed it couldn't be a siren or anything that sounded like cops or an ambulance. I argued for Gregorian chants and Joe held out for "Ave Maria."

At our destination, our joking stopped. "That's not freon, it's ammonia," I said as we exited the car, "—and that could seriously kill somebody."

All around us, life was proceeding as usual. At a food stall across the narrow street from the ice house people ignored the bad smell and spooned up bowls of noodle soup. How unusual, after all, was an offensive odor in a Bangkok slum?

Joe accessed the situation and we took off at a trot toward the Mercy Centre, where, after he was assured that everything was alright, he left me with a friend. Bangkok is one of those unusual cities where personal safety was pretty much assured everywhere and at all times, but Joe insisted that unless you were Thai, Klong Toey had not only bad smells, but also the whiff of danger for out-

siders. As a longtime resident known in the neighborhood, he figured he was exempt from any such threat.

As I waited for Joe to return, I remembered how he'd come
to Bangkok in 1967, straight from seminary in California, to say
Mass to American soldiers fighting the war in Vietnam. His
grandparents were homesteaders farming wheat in what was
then called the Dakota Territory. His parents—German father,
Irish mother—ran a whorehouse in Chicago for a while and after
Joe was born, his dad became a fisherman on the West Coast, a
ship's captain running supplies for the army to the Aleutian
Islands during World War II, a truck driver in Washington state,
a farmer back in South Dakota, a traveling salesman, a guitar-
playing minstrel, a house painter, a womanizer, an absent father
and a drunk.

Joe's younger sister and brother were born in the harsh
Dakota winter and both times, at age ten and twelve, Joe drove
the tractor, pulling the car behind him with his mom and dad in
it until they reached the county highway, where they waited for a
snowplow to clear a path into town, so that his siblings could be
born in a hospital. He milked cows. Ran a threshing machine.
Finally, the old man just sort of disappeared and when Joe went
to catechism summer camp, classmates laughed at his clothing,
one pair of high-top work shoes and two pairs of bib overalls.

Eventually, his parents divorced, and his mom and the kids settled in Washington state where she had a sister and found a job
as a secretary; welfare took up the slack. Joe's mother was a strong
woman, Joe said—manipulative, larger than life; "I had my first
adult conversation with her when I was fifty-three."

Starting in the seventh grade, Joe was shipped off to a Catholic
seminary in California for six years, during which time he became
the only Eagle Scout in the seminary. He was mercilessly teased,
just as he was a target in the troop for being the only Catholic. He
also suffered through a bout of polio that affected some minor

muscles in his face and made his fingers unfit for continuing piano lessons, although he was still able to make a fist.

After a spiritual internship in Missouri, Joe was ordained and shipped off to another seminary in Wisconsin. This is where he earned his merit badge in rebellion, challenging seminary regulations and protesting the nascent Vietnam war. His superiors got their revenge. In 1967, as the war heated up, they sent him to the country next to it, Thailand. He was not pleased. And he vowed not to stay.

"I was an angry young man," he recalled, "and the rest of the priests were glad to see the back of me."

The sermons on the military bases stopped when he completed his Thai language classes and was posted in Loei near the Laos border, where he taught himself Lao, and then, after crossing into Laos, took his faith to the hilltribes; he once told me he thought he still could say Mass in Hmong. This is when he got to know all the classic characters—and killers—of the secret Laos war.

By war's end, Joe was back in Bangkok, where he took over the parish in the city's toughest slum, called the Slaughterhouse for the abattoir where three thousand pigs were killed every night. Most of the butchers were descended from Vietnamese Catholics who migrated to Thailand, because Buddhists were forbidden to kill and Muslims wouldn't go near pork. Fast food joints refused to deliver in this neighborhood, taxis wouldn't take you there after dark, and if you let it slip to a prospective employer that you lived there, you didn't get hired. Joe moved into a two-room shanty squat in the middle of the slum, slept on an old army cot, dressed himself out of the poor box, offered spiritual nourishment to the butchers and their families, and in 1972, started a kindergarten. This is where the accomplishments that followed began. From then on, Joe said, it was war, and the priest not only said Mass on the weekend, he became an urban guerilla.

When he heard a ten-year-old girl whose mother was a prostitute in a brothel was going to introduce the girl to the trade, Joe negotiated a price with the brothel owner to buy the girl, then put her in a school and a foster home. When a twelve-year-old slum girl was raped and a man was apprehended, it looked as if he'd walk after paying a bribe. Joe had four hundred slum women march on the police station, telling the cops to either guarantee they'd prosecute the sonofabitch or give him to the women for one hour, and if they didn't do one or the other, he'd be back the next day with the women *and* media. (The man was sentenced to seven years.) When Joe learned that some gangs were planning a move on a neighborhood and he noticed that the canine population was nil, he organized a posse and "borrowed" a dozen or so animals from another slum area to stand guard.

Perhaps he was most creative when there was a fire. They averaged about two a year, and Joe believed that it was important to rebuild immediately. A community meeting was held even as the embers cooled. The city had a program where homeowners—even if they were squatters living on land illegally—were entitled to more than $500 after a fire, and renters got about half of that. Joe said he'd advance the money needed to start construction on an adjacent piece of wasteland that very day, explaining that the longer they delayed, the harder it would be to claim the right to rebuild on or adjacent to the original slum site.

Joe's social workers told the people that after a fire, everything material was gone, except for the few items saved on the way out of the flames, so it was important to hold on to the social structure. That meant that if these people could continue to send their children to the same schools, if they could continue to take the same bus routes to their jobs, if they could continue to shop at the same slum stores, if they could continue to see the friends and relatives with whom they'd lived—often for generations—still in place as a community, their chances of survival were increased. And the psychological damage might be diminished.

At the meeting, they also were told that the new houses probably would be smaller than their old ones and that it would take a year, maybe two years, fighting through all the red tape before they could rebuild on their original sites. It would not be easy. At one such meeting I attended, a man said if rebuilding was illegal, maybe the police would arrest them. He was told that if anyone were arrested, everyone else in the neighborhood was to go to the police station and surrender, confessing identical guilt. Before they went, the mommies were to give the children as much to drink as possible and sticky candy to eat, so that when they got to the police station the smallest children would end up peeing on the floor and leaving their gummy handprints on policemen's trousers. The mommies were also told to have the children take their dogs, so they could pee on the floor as well.

Committees were formed. One to deal with the police and government. Another to distribute food and clothing that was coming in from the business sector and concerned citizens. A third to organize activities for the children. One more to visit the lumber yards the next day and find the cheapest nails and wood and corrugated roofing, all at Joe's expense, repayment due when the government honored its mandated compensation.

The fire meeting I attended was on Thursday afternoon. The lumber and so on was delivered by Friday night. Construction began right away. Daddies, mommies and children carried the boards and bags of cement. Tools were loaned by others in the slum. The nine-meter-long poles that would be used as corner posts for the new homes were too long to be carried down the twisting walkways from the highway, so the men waded across a swamp with the boards on their backs.

All night and through the next two days and nights the slum echoed with the sounds of hammers and saws. Every slum has its "slum carpenters"—men who have worked in construction or who have built their own homes in the past—and they told the others what to do. No one slept longer than a few hours, thanks in part to someone's having laced the drinking water with amphetamines.

The last family moved into the last house at 6:30 a.m. Monday, just as the sun came up and well before government offices came to life in an effort to keep the slum dwellers from rebuilding. The stench of the charred wood still hung in the air, along with the sweet smell of success.

In every war there are losses as well as victories and Joe's was no different. Pigs were not slaughtered on a monthly occurrence called Monks' Day, but on one of them, which also happened to be his birthday, Joe arrived at the Slaughterhouse in his white robes, coming from some public appearance. He stopped to lead the butchers and their families, who lived in shacks built on top of the killing pens, in saying the rosary. Nearby was a small group of men who'd decided to kill some pigs anyway, for the easy profit, and they ignored Joe when he asked them to stop for the twelve minutes that the prayers took. In response, the men splashed Joe with warm blood. He was shocked. He remembered bolting and then standing still, alone, for five minutes, then joining another group of men who customarily spent their evenings drinking and gossiping. Joe told them what happened and said he was going back to America.

Packing a small bag, he drove to the Holy Redeemer Church and, finding it locked up for the night, climbed a drainpipe in the back and went to sleep in one of the small bedrooms usually used by new or visiting priests. About three in the morning, he was awakened by a pounding on the church door. He pulled on some clothes and to his great surprise, he saw several of the Slaughterhouse men, drunk, who'd arrived in a pickup truck. "You can come home now," one of them said. "We took care of the problem." Joe was told that when the police arrived to arrest the men for violating Monks' Day, mysteriously they'd all had accidents and had broken arms and legs. Eleven were taken to the hospital and the owner of the firm that employed the men was taken to the police station and told it would cost him $2,000 if he wanted to go home.

Another time, when a young priest in the slum was threatened—he later became an archbishop—one of Joe's neighbors (now deceased) carved up the would-be assailant and fed him to the fish in the polluted canal that ran alongside the Slaughterhouse.

"It's war," Joe said. "The slums never invited me. I walked in and said here I am, let the Klong Toey wars begin. It was total arrogance and bravado. I tend to overstate and over-emotionalize, but I'm right. We've never done anything legal, but we've always played it straight, we've never broken the rules of the street." He paused and then talked about a bishop in Brazil who told him, "When I help the poor, they call me a saint, and when I teach the poor how to help themselves, they call me a communist." Joe paused again and finished his small speech: "I'd rather be a communist."

For twenty-five years, he was the only priest who visited Bangkok's meanest prisons. He also conducted Mass every Sunday for a quarter century at the prestigious Asian Institute of Technology, from which he also received, following a year's study, a degree in urban development. After a while, he incorporated his foundation (in the church's name, of course), and by 2003, he had built more than ten thousand slum houses of his own design and was riding herd on thirty-three schools with an enrolment of 4,500 kids and more than seventy thousand "graduates" who'd learned the basics of literacy (from teachers who were born in the same slums); five shelters for over two hundred orphaned, abandoned and abused children; the city's oldest AIDS hospice for fifty children and 150 adults; social workers on the street seven days a week; a legal attack team that represented two hundred kids in courts and police stations every month; a twenty-four-hour medical clinic, a credit union and women's advocacy group; and several self-help, skill-teaching programs that produced everything from candles to Christmas cards.

As I remembered all this, I stood near the compound that included the AIDS hospice, two of the shelters, the largest school and the foundation's offices, a $4-million fortress called the Mercy Centre, financed by an American businessman from Atlanta.

As I ruminated, Joe told me later, he arrived at the neighborhood police station, where for the next twenty minutes the portly, balding, sixty-year-old priest from South Dakota, whose mixed Irish and German blood boiled at thirty degrees Celsius, the average daily temperature in Bangkok, informed the cops who had the misfortune to be on duty that night precisely how they were fucking up. (His words.)

Why weren't any cops on the scene at the ice house? He wanted to know. Why didn't they have a loudspeaker announcing the danger from inhaling ammonia gas? Was anything being done about the leak? Did they know how harmful ammonia was? What was the plan if someone got sick?

There were many cops who welcomed Joe, and there were others who liked to get rid of him as quickly as possible, even if they had to capitulate a little, so in a short time, it was agreed that the police would dispatch someone to the ice house with one of those battery-operated megaphones and search for any injured or ill, in the plant and in the immediate neighborhood, and if any were found, to take them to the hospital.

After collecting me, Joe and I hot-footed it back to the ice house, where he confronted the owner, who was sitting nonchalantly on the loading dock. The smell of ammonia was still noxious in the air.

Now, Joe gave *her* holy hell, causing her to lose a bit of her face as there were several others present, but extracting a promise to pay for any possible hospital costs.

With the cops arriving and the woman moving to greet them,

Joe and I returned to his car. "This," he said as we walked, "is how journalists and priests get killed."

I laughed again. "Happy New Year to you, too, Joe."

Ménage à Trois

I wasn't the first foreigner to build a home in Nam Bua Daeng. Ron Hutchinson, a Scot, was there before me, marrying and building a two-story house for my wife Lamyai's closest frend, Jeab, an abandoned mother of two who'd met Ron at the same Three Roses bar where I later met Lamyai. He also bought her a pickup truck, taught her how to drive and sent a monthly allowance from the comfortable sum he earned working in Saudi Arabia.

Jeab was six years younger than Lamyai and about two-thirds her size, a spunky little thing with a firecracker personality. She also drank and was addicted to a card game called "hi-lo." But she was not, entirely, a layabout. Nam Bua Daeng was more a "hamlet" than a village, without a store or a place to eat, so once she quit the bar business, Jeab erected two rows of shelves beneath a roof, lined them with the basics—dry noodle soup, soaps and shampoo, batteries and light bulbs, cooking oil, whisky, a selection of pharmaceuticals, snacks and candy and cigarettes—and stocked a standup, glass-fronted fridge with soda and the cheapest brand of beer. She also moved in a tank of gas and set up a three-burner, outdoor kitchen, preparing soups and stir-fries every day, priced at the equivalent of 25 US cents. It helped pay for the gambling.

At first, Ron was someone who visited Thailand on holidays. He didn't gamble, but he smoked and drank voluminously, so it was no surprise when he was disabled by a diseased liver and emphysema and his employer retired him at age fifty-nine. At about the same time Lamyai and I moved into our new home, he began fulltime residence in Nam Bua Daeng.

It wasn't easy for them. Ron's money and belongings were still tied up in Saudi Arabia and he continued to drink and smoke and an earlier hip replacement acted up and he was reduced to using a walker for a while. Even when he recovered, he did little more than sit in a chair in the little "store/kitchen" and make change while smoking, drinking and watching football on TV. While Jeab played cards between selling bowls of rice and soup.

Sometimes, Jeab said she'd stop gambling if Ron gave up the booze. Sometimes it was the other way around. But then one of them would backslide and all hell broke loose. Once, Jeab bit into Ron's left arm, leaving the crescent marks of her teeth as a permanent scar. Another time, when he passed out in the middle of an argument, she was so angry she shaved him bald. The villagers, whose homes were only a few meters away, were delighted; it gave them something to talk about.

All that said, I really believed that Ron and Jeab cared about each other, that their shared spousal abuse—the "boxing," as Lamyai called it—was their way of showing love. They also kept few secrets about their mutually enjoyed time in bed together, providing further entertainment for those living within hearing.

Still, Ron never really got into being a resident of Nam Bua Daeng. He knew only a little more Thai than I did and didn't like Thai food, insisting that Jeab prepare the meat and starch dishes that sustained him all his life. He refused to visit the monks' encampment in the woods. Aside from Jeab and her daughters, I was his only friend, and a one-week-a-month pal at that. His house had the only telephone land line in the village and he enjoyed sending and receiving e-mail. The last time we talked, he asked me to bring some new software for Jeab's oldest daughter, for whom he had bought a computer. He taught her how to use it, thus making her the only computer-literate Thai in miles.

The next time I went home to Nam Bua Daeng, he was dead. Lamyai and I visited Jeab and she showed us photographs of Ron, curled in eternal sleep; an autopsy showed his liver had beaten his lungs to the final punch as he slept. Over the desk where he once sat making change, Jeab had erected a small shrine, with his photograph, flowers, incense and a glass of beer.

Lamyai and I accompanied Jeab to visit the monks and after arranging some fresh flowers in Ron's memory, she asked if we wanted to "see" Ron. She retrieved a sealed vase from one side of the altar and said it contained his ashes. She then produced the two titanium parts of Ron's artificial hip that hadn't melted during the cremation and clinked them together. "Ron not come here before he die," she said, "–now he here forever!"

Within a few months, after selling his computers–Ron's money and goods were still in Saudi Arabia–Jeab hung up her rubber slippers and took out her dancing shoes and returned to work in a bar in Bangkok. Her fifteen-year-old daughter wanted to be a flight attendant and that meant she had to continue her education and learn to speak English fluently.

That was in December. In May, 2002, a forty-five-year-old, yellow-haired, rosy-cheeked, corpulent bus driver from Denmark named Villy Danborg entered the Three Roses Bar, met Jeab, and spent the next four days with her in a hotel room across the street. They communicated in English–"Ve talk, ve make luf," he later told me–and before returning to Copenhagen, he asked Jeab to marry him. In the months that followed, he wrote long letters (which I read to her) and they talked on the phone as often as a dozen times a day. In this way, Jeab learned that he had twin nine-teen-year-old sons by a Danish woman he never married, a five-year-old son by a Vietnamese woman he did marry. Both women walked out on him—also leaving their sons behind—as did a sub-sequent Thai wife, aged forty, who migrated to Denmark under his sponsorship with a teenaged son; she left Villy and moved in with a man only a little more than half her age soon afterward, taking her son with her. This left Villy with three boys to raise and he said they, and he, needed a woman.

Through persistence, Villy convinced Jeab to get a passport and visa to visit Denmark for three months. The idea was that if it worked out, they'd then get married and Jeab's two daughters would move to Copenhagen, too. (During her initial visit, her daughters were to remain in Thailand with her brother.) Villy said he wasn't rich, but his salary, plus a fee for managing the forty-unit co-op in which he had a spacious flat, gave him $4,000 after taxes a month and he thought they could live on it comfortably, while Jeab's girls could get a western education.

On a later visit to Thailand to meet Jeab's family and visit her village (and then accompany Jeab home with him), Lamyai and I helped Jeab through the passport and visa process and told Villy we'd accompany him on the overnight train to Surin. I also offered to help him try to understand the strange new world that he was about to experience. I liked Villy. I thought he was an innocent as well as a romantic, and if I thought he was rushing things, he had a good heart and when he said, "I luf her, I cannot help myself," I knew he meant it.

The village came as a shock, I think. He was pleased by the modern house that Ron built, and impressed by ours, as well, but the village's engulfing shabbiness, trash strewn everywhere, everything tired and worn, the women doing little more than gos-sip all day, the men drinking from early morning, nobody doing much work, left Villy quite distressed, especially after seeing

Lamyai's extensive and flourishing gardens. Why didn't the others do the same? I told Villy about the "inertia of the poor," a concept that generally applied to the poorest of the poor, those who had, more or less, given up or lost any desire for or notion of improvement, taking whatever came. Westerners might confuse this with what they, the foreigners, called laziness.

Notice, too, I said, that most of the people in the village were old or very young. The middle generation, the parents of many of the children he saw, worked elsewhere, many of them in Bangkok, because there was no money here. I said I knew of seven households (out of about forty) in Nam Bua Daeng whose young women either worked in the bars or returned home only after a *farang* started sending money. What he and I did, I said, contributed much to Thailand's rural economy. The war bride phenomenon didn't begin with American hostilities in Vietnam, but it flourished then and spread to Thailand and the Philippines, where few of the brides were met in a church. Thousands of foreign men married Thai bargirls and took them home, while others remained in Thailand with them, or didn't marry them but wired regular allowances to their bank accounts. There was an old joke about the *farang* being taken home and the woman saying, "I'd like you to meet your village-in-law."

Meanwhile, Jeab was behaving in a manner that seemed designed to offend, as if she were trying to get Villy to change his mind. She told me that she was tipsy when she met him at the airport and hadn't completely sobered up since. She was smoking ganja, too, and filling up her mouth with the blood-red mix of leaves and paste and bark and betel nut that she sometimes chewed. His determination and cheerfulness never faltered, his "luf" untouched by her boorish assault.

"I have this determination and cheerfulness because the angel talked to me," Villy told me some time later. "Just ten minutes before I saw Jeab the first time, the angel told me that I now will meet one girl I can stay together with. I wrote in my diary that she was the most bad girl in all Nana Plaza. But I loved her and I trusted the voice in my head, telling me not to be afraid."

The second day of Villy's visit to Nam Bua Daeng a small party was planned to formally introduce him to neighbors and family members; few of the latter lived nearby, or even often talked. (Another disturbing factor for Villy, after he and Jeab came to see us the previous evening, finding Lamyai's entire family—siblings, their kids, the lot—sitting in a big circle sharing a meal.) Lamyai and I arrived at Jeab's house at ten, dressed in expensive, tailored silk, appearing sartorially apart from but mixing easily with the other guests, few of whom even bothered to find a clean tee-shirt (one of which was emblazoned with Osama bin Laden's face). It was loud and chaotic and the storehouse of beer and whisky was rapidly depleted; Jeab dispatched someone to a nearby town for more and soon the men were pissing in the yard.

That was when Villy delivered his bombshell. Just that morning, he told me, Jeab said she would marry him and the monks were arriving at eleven. Did this mean they were getting married—today? Villy said yes, and he was thrilled, of course. He said he'd never married an alcoholic before and he thought it would be interesting. He said he drank two to five beers every night, but he had a rule: no alcohol was to be consumed in the house during the day and one of his nineteen-year-old sons was there to enforce it. What of Jeab? I asked. What was she to do while he drove his bus? He said she'd find something. He said there was a woman from Phnom Penh she might get to know, another bargirl who'd married a Dane; he was disappointed when I told him that the Khmer Jeab spoke was so different she would not be able to talk to the Cambodian.

The four monks arrived, taking seats in a row on futons along one wall, about thirty of us sat on our feet before them, and the string-blessing ceremony began, accompanied by what seemed like hours of monotonous chanting. I won't recount all the details of the complex Thai-Khmer ritual except to say that it was as almost as weird as the house blessing that took place when Lamyai and I built our home. My favorite image: a pig's head placed before an altar, still leaking blood from its noisy, early morning demise, a lighted candle projecting from one side of its piggy lips like a cigarette in Humphrey Bogart's mouth.

After the ceremony, Lamyai accompanied Jeab to the regional government office to register the marriage. Villy introduced me to the village headman and said he and another neighbor had to make written statements affirming that Ron was dead; the photos and death certificate apparently weren't enough. I asked Villy if he knew that any of this was planned—and, in fact, already under way—when he woke up that morning. He said he had not. But, he added, "I get goot feelings. Life iss a surprise, iss it not?"

I wondered why she'd done it. I knew that the ceremony, even the *tambon* registration meant nothing in Denmark and that for her to remain there, and bring her children, a Danish marriage was required. Perhaps the ritual and attendant legalities that she arranged here were no more than performance, to prove to her neighbors as well as to herself that she was still desirable. Another unkind thought? I hope so, but I find it difficult to believe Jeab did it to make Villy happy. It certainly didn't please her daughter, who still clung to Ron's memory and was in school during the ceremony.

Jeab's sudden action seemed precipitous to me, but I'm sure she didn't do it to spite her daughter or (at least not entirely) to "moon" her neighbors. She didn't love Ron at first, after all; it was something that came later, as did Lamyai's love for me. What I prefer to believe is that Jeab could be as much of a romantic as is Villy. Both want the very same thing, and both are coming from need. Millions of other relationships have been founded, then foundered or flourished with no more to provide support.

At the party following the ceremony, Villy continued to play the gracious host, pouring the champagne he'd brought from Denmark, topping up the neighbors' drinks, telling everyone, "*Chok dee!*"

"*Skol*, Villy!" I said, draining the last of my beer.

The next night, Jeab and Villy returned to Bangkok and a day after that they went to Denmark, where Jeab and Villy soon were married in a town hall. Then, on her first return visit to Thailand, she obtained visas for her children and earned a certificate in traditional Thai massage at the oldest temple in Bangkok, returning to Copenhagen to open her own business. She also quit drinking—"vell, maybe one, two glass vine at the end uff the day," said Villy—and devoted her newfound energy to her business, which apparently was an immediate success. There is a song that says dreams come true in blue Hawaii. So, too, they come true in Bangkok, as well as in Denmark.

Professor Elephant

It's Richard Lair's favorite portrait. Standing in an old teak forest in Thailand, dressed in white tie and tails, he raises his baton to conduct an orchestra. But this isn't an ordinary orchestra. All the musicians are elephants.

When that photograph appeared in *People* magazine, it marked the conclusion of recording sessions that led to the first of two commercially released CDs, Richard's latest scheme to raise money to save the endangered Asian elephant.

He admits that the plot was alcohol-inspired when on one of his rare visits to the United States, he met and spent an evening drinking with David Sulzer, a New York biochemist who moonlighted as an *avant garde* musician, using the name David Soldier. This was in 1999, a year after Richard joined the Thai Elephant Conservation Centre in Lampang in northern Thailand. The project was the offshoot of an earlier stunt, launched when two Russian artists approached Richard, asking if they could teach his animals to paint. When the colorful results were auctioned by Christie's for more than $90,000, the cynicism that greeted the idea quickly waned. So, too, when he proposed taking some of the earnings from the art project to make elephant-sized musical instruments.

Rail thin, mustachioed, his face lined like an elephant's hide from a lifetime of heavy smoking, with a voice that sounds like TV host Dick Cavett's, and known in Thailand as Acharn Chang, or Professor Elephant, Richard is the man who found and trained the elephants for Disney's *Operation Dumbo Drop* and served as pachyderm advisor for Oliver Stone's feature film about Alexander the Great; the author of the definitive work on the domesticated Asian elephant, *Gone Astray,* who now is co-authoring a handbook for *mahouts*, the native elephant trainers, and employees of Asia's growing number of elephant camps. When it comes to the Asian elephant, he is regarded as one of the world's unchallenged authorities.

Having worked with the Asian pachyderm for most of his adult life, he agrees with animal rights advocates who say elephants should not be forced to mimic human activities. The argument goes along the lines that, because domesticated elephants have never been selectively bred, and are both genetically and behaviorally wild, they simply shouldn't even be in captivity, much less forced to make music. Environmental degradation has removed most of Thailand's natural forest and without forage, the animals would starve in the wild, anyway, or make pests of themselves raiding farms.

"However sad it might be," Richard says, "virtually all elephants in Thailand must work for a living. All our musicians perform for visitors in several shows daily, where they demonstrate traditional timber work wearing the very symbol of slavery, a logging harness. So, being able to bang on musical instruments and make gorgeous noises of their own volition—and invention—is at worst soft duty and for most of them it's clearly a great pleasure. Yes, the elephants are unjustly incarcerated, but what better job than to be in the prison band?

"Yes, we're exploiting elephants, but it's for their own good and we've exploited elephants for four thousand years not for their own good. Nowadays in Thailand, where logging is illegal and elephants are no longer needed for transportation, tourism is the only real source of work. And the CDs we're producing are sold to help pay their keep."

The animals are lined up behind a row of outsized instruments—sturdy drums and cymbals, a gong fashioned appropriately from an old lumber saw blade, xylophones made from iron pipes, which the elephants play with mallets held in their trunks. (Experiments with harmonicas got mixed results as they tended to get clogged with elephant drool; the early sounds were great, but they wore out quickly.) Richard worked out a set of hand signals for the *mahouts* to cue the elephants while he was conducting, discovering that some of the animals "figured out the meaning of the signals on their own, with no teaching whatsoever." That said, whatever happens, happens; Lair admits it is difficult to get a musician that weighs three tons to stop if the animal is really into it.

Richard adds, more seriously, that "the surprisingly sparse research into elephant intelligence has always utilized sight as the testing medium even though the elephant's hearing, along with its ability to smell, is a far more acute sense. Therefore, some of the tools and knowledge gained in making music might lead to a better way to do some real science."

Richard says his earliest memory was looking at an elephant in the San Francisco Zoo when he was two- or three-years old. A bout of polio as a boy that left him with one leg shorter than the other kept him in a hospital or at home for two years and "when I was really depressed, I'd get on a bus and go to the zoo and sit there looking at the Asian elephants. I read every book I could about elephants and drew pictures of them."

He did two years of pre-med at San Francisco State University and dropped out, went to Europe to paint, traveled in Asia, then returned to northern California to study filmmaking and work as a cinematographer on several nature documentaries. That's when he developed an interest in endangered species, finding little scientific information about Asian elephants. After working as an apprentice trainer for eight months at Marine World Africa in California, in the early 1970s he spent two years studying wild elephants in Southern India and with permission to study elephants in another part of India, he made a short detour to Bangkok before starting his new assignment. Armed tribal struggles erupted, however, and his permission to return to India was withdrawn. He's been in Thailand ever since and "because one leg was short," he says, "I accepted the fact that I would not be able to run from a charging elephant in the wild and that I was safer studying domestic ones."

He taught himself to speak and read Thai, starting by memorizing folk sayings and poetry and, once, for more than two years he lived with *mahouts* in the jungle, developing a tolerance if not a taste for the sometimes unusual local diet, including warm blood in the morning instead of coffee and insects for an afternoon snack.

I met Richard when he lived in Bangkok when I was researching a story about foreign filmmaking in Thailand. (He told me that the star of *Operation Dumbo Drop* was flown in from the U.S. and because the elephant's system wasn't used to the local water, a flat-bed truck load of bottled water was delivered every day; imagine, he said, an elephant with diarrhea.) We became good friends, collaborated on magazine articles, and after he moved to up north, I visited him there, and we got together when he came to Bangkok. In between, we talked every week at least once on the phone and exchanged paperback novels by mail, books about cops and lawyers and crooks, the sort of reading matter he called "paper television." He also is well-read in more literary circles and by the early 1990s his Thai was so good he translated from Thai to English a novel about a *mahout* and his animal, *High Banks*,

Heavy Logs by Nikom Rayawa; his translation, published by Penguin in Australia, was as acclaimed as the book itself.

One of my visits with Richard coincided with the treatment at the Friends of the Asian Elephant's hospital of a thirty-eight-year-old cow named Motola injured by a land mine in Burma. The animal had been walked through the jungle for two days by villagers to the nearest road, where she was loaded onto a truck and then driven a hundred miles to Lampang. At the hospital, veterinarians removed the most severely damaged flesh and eventually a prosthetic device was fashioned to the stump.

More trouble lay ahead. With Motola placing so much weight on her opposite front foot, one toenail and the footpad started splitting off. Richard told me it was impossible to treat this wound and that it could result in Motola being lame in both front feet. Although this second wound hadn't been publicized, the hospital was getting letters from Western veterinarians asking why the animal wasn't "put down."

"How could we?" Richard said. "After all the care and concern of the villagers in getting her here? And she's not a troublesome patient. In fact, she's unusually intelligent and gentle. If she'd been a belligerent, aggressive animal, as many are, we might've said the hell with her and been less inclined to go to so much trouble. But look at her eyes. You *know* she's intelligent."

As we talked, someone arrived with a big armload of palm leaves and when Motola began eating her lunch, we went on to look at a young elephant that'd been brought in dehydrated and suffering from a diet of Coca Cola and junk food after being kept in a hotel in southern Thailand. The animal was only eighteen months old, Richard said, and in the wild a mother elephant weans her calf at three years. The elephant's ribs showed through its gray flank and the spine stood in sharp relief.

"Elephant problems all come from association with man," Richard said. "Without us, they'd be just fine."

It's not surprising that Richard is a loner, preferring to spend his evenings and weekends at home with a bottle of "sipping whisky" (his brand of choice, Jack Daniels) and his collection of seven hundred or so music tapes—heavy on ethnic sounds, from Cajun to Cambodian, a collection so complete that when I visited with my wife, who is Thai but ethnically Khmer, he played the recordings that she listened to as a child.

One of my favorite memories is watching Richard listening to a funky blues tune, eyes closed, glass in one hand, the other weaving overhead as he danced, his movement unimpaired by his bum leg. High? Maybe. Happy? Clearly.

He has a television set, but rarely turns it on it, getting most of his news from BBC World Radio.

Some say Richard prefers the company of animals, and he once told me that if he had his way, he'd buy a "cabin at the bend of some river" and never have anything much again to do with either man or beast.

As for those pachyderm CDs, despite the fact that they inspired some groaning journalistic word play ("Thailand's Big Band Sound," "Jumbo Jamming," "Keep on Trunkin'", etc.) and from one writer an unflattering comparison to Yoko Ono, the *New York Times* included it on its "Best of the Obscure Albums" list and most critics regarded it seriously. Some of it was repetitious, it wasn't easy to dance to, and the occasional trumpeting that the world's largest land mammal added spontaneously was no threat to the haunting voice of the ocean's largest mammal, the whale. Yet, it also was called "New Age with a Thai religious touch" by one periodical, while others noted the elephant's ability to distinguish fine pitch changes. The *New York Times* called the recordings "at once meditative and deliberate, delicate and distinctly thrumming..."

Amazon.com's classical music editor Jason Verlinde said, "All of it is entertaining, but the human-led tracks just can't compete with the inventive elephants and their ragged, slow-paced, and off-kilter music-making. Granted, you probably won't want to hear Phrathida, JoJo, and Luuk Kob pounding away every day, but the elephants probably feel the same way about Cecil Taylor."

Richard's partner Dave Soldier proposed giving the music the Turing test of artificial intelligence, devised to determine whether a computer possesses intelligence. "Try playing the recording to people without telling them the identity of the performers and then ask them if it's music. They may love it or they may beg you to stop, but I think they will say, 'Of course it's music.' And they won't ever guess that the band weighs more than a herd of Buicks."

To which, Richard gives his grinning assent and adds, "Besides, it's the best music ever produced by Thai civil servants."

Caveman

Since 1989, when John Gray founded a company called SeaCanoe Thailand Inc. and introduced commercial kayaking to Thailand, he says he's been victimized by racism; harassed by the government on trumped-up drug and immigration charges; assaulted, robbed and betrayed by employees; and strong-armed by the murderous local "birds' nest mafia," all while watching the environment, in which he tried to paddle so calmly, ravaged by rampant and uncaring competition. He even saw one of his key employees shot three times in front of his office and in his unlucky thirteenth year finally was squeezed out of the business. Why, one wonders, does he stay?

Maybe it's because he's won so much acclaim for his efforts to promote honest eco-tourism, receiving five international awards including one from *Smithsonian* magazine. Maybe it's because he respects nature so much and believes so fervently in the possibilities of green tourism. And maybe, just maybe, it's because the six-foot-four-inch former footballer from the United States simply enjoys the fight.

"Don't call us a tour company!" John said when I interviewed him for a magazine in 1995, when his company was at the top of its form and there were only a few competitors taking tourists into the sea caves in Phang Nga Bay. "We are not a tour company. I don't even like the word 'eco-tourism.' Adventure travel, maybe. This is a back-to-nature trip, a chance to go back in time, where everything is still the way it was before you and I showed up."

The first widespread attention given the tall, oddly shaped islands that formed the focus of his business was when the bay was a setting for the James Bond thriller, *The Man With the Golden Gun*, starring Roger Moore in 1974. All the maps John obtained when he came to Phuket a decade later showed the islands were solid, but during his explorations he discovered that many were not. While circling one, he noticed a cave and paddled into it. Seeing daylight at the end of a serpentine tunnel that led off the cave, he entered a secret lagoon, called a *hong*, the Thai word for room.

What John had stumbled into had been created by the erosion and collapse of the centers of ancient limestone pillars, leaving vertical chimneys open to light and rain that, in time, nourished an ecosystem that now included trees and plants, monkeys, birds, reptiles and insects, and in the lagoons a rich variety of fish and other marine life. Entry was through caverns decorated with oyster-encrusted rock gardens, stalactites, and shimmering limestone waterfalls, or tunnels so small passengers had to lie flat in the canoes, the stone roofs only centimeters from their noses as they slipped through at extreme low tide. Flooded during high tides, visitors needed to get in and out fast and have someone who knew when and how to do that.

"Each time I paddled into a new *hong*," John said, "I wondered if I might encounter a salt water crocodile. They were considered extinct, but what I found was so primitive, so pristine, I honestly thought it was a possibility."

He never made such a discovery, but that didn't halt this becoming John Gray's time machine, his paddle into the prehistoric past, packaged for visitors for about $100 a piece per day, an adventure that included a visit to a sea gypsy village on stilts and a gourmet seafood lunch prepared aboard the escort ship from the catch of passing fishermen.

I took the day trip twice and later went on a three-day, two-night excursion, ranking it miles ahead of Thailand's whitewater rafting and hilltribe treks or anything else offered with the word "nature" or "ethnic" or "eco-" attached. Sliding through the first *hong* John explored, called Bat Cave for its numerous furry inhabitants, and then back into daylight onto the surface of a placid lake with jungled walls rising hundreds of meters to a china blue sky was, if not to return to prehistory, at least a return to childhood, when innocence and awe were still intact.

I was impressed by the Thai guides' environmental awareness, too; not only were they able to identify and talk (in several languages) about the wild life we encountered, they collected floating trash and enforced silence once we'd entered a cave. "This, to me, is a temple," John said, "made by God. Man cannot make a temple as sacred as these places are and if we come, we should have a minimal impact, and there should be a specific purpose for it."

In the years that followed, John and I became friends, despite the fact that he wrote a "painstakingly detailed" (his words) letter about my article that made it clear that, in his view, I was full of shit. My story was assigned by a Thai business magazine and that was the approach I took: John Gray as a businessman. What I didn't realize then was that he wasn't one, or at least not the usual one.

Surely he didn't look like one. Hair "receding from a sloping simian forehead"–quoting *Outside* magazine–"and a grungy beard smeared across his chops, he's the incarnation of Grog, star of the comic strip B.C." Fittingly, the nickname given him by the Hash House Harriers was "Caveman."

Mind you, he read all the right people and spouted all the correct phrases. Ed Deming, the American quality-control guru who told the Japanese how to beat the U.S. at its own game, was John's idol. He was also a dedicated environmental and social activist who went roaring into Phuket with a notion that he described as a "development exercise" designed to "help rural villagers achieve self-determination, economic sustainability and scientific aware-ness." For this, he retained only nineteen percent ownership—thirty percent less than most foreign joint venture partners—the rest given to four Thai partners who contributed "not cash, but sweat equity." And the company was an immediate success.

John grew up in Los Angeles in the 1950s, the son of a dentist who took his son to Dodgers games and then on water-skiing trips to Catalina Island on the weekends, guiding him through SCUBA certification at age twelve, and setting his life pattern as a jock and ardent outdoorsman, a 110-kilogram (242-pound) hulk who, while playing varsity ball at UCLA, could run forty yards in four-and-a-half seconds. Yet, to hear him tell it, it was his mom who had the greater influence. A feisty woman who openly opposed Japanese internment in the U.S. during World War II and in 1953, when her husband was called back into the service to serve in a M.A.S.H unit in Korea, she was the only officer's wife who agreed to live in traditional Japanese housing, while all the others lived, by choice, in military shoeboxes. She also defied the Army by taking her Japanese maid to the officers' club.

"This was the attitude I grew up with," John says.

After service in the Navy—John wanted to be a SEAL, but was told to edit training manuals instead—and a few seasons of semi-pro football, he washed up on Oahu's north shore in the mid-1970s with his hair grown out and a fondness for bodysurfing and battling the establishment. A noisy environmentalist whose efforts helped kill a $2-billion real estate development, he told me his partners in a kayaking firm there cleaned him out while he was exploring the Thai islands, stealing everything except his boats. With the money earned from final expeditions in Hawaii and Fiji and contributions from a half-dozen friends, including his ex-wife, he packed his boats (his own design which, when deflated, fit into airplane-friendly suitcases) and returned to Phuket.

Initially, it went well, and there seemed to be caves enough for all, even when, by the time I wrote my story, some of John's employees had left to start their own companies and SeaCanoe had been called to a meeting with the local mafia chief and told—after a .45 pistol had been placed on the table—that he was to give up fifty percent of his company. John refused and, to his surprise, he heard nothing further. SeaCanoe also survived the arrest of the company's *farang* business manager on a cannabis charge. John insists the man was framed, but really all that mattered in the end was that the company put up the bail and the man fled, thus wiping out the company's cash account. Later, John himself was arrested for collecting a loan and signing a marketing agreement, business activity forbidden without a government work permit. On another occasion, an employee stole ten boats and held them for ransom; John eventually paid.

Despite these problems, SeaCanoe flourished, fueled in part by John's sincere rhetoric. Just as his untrimmed beard and big motorcycle and aging hippie image sometimes worked against him in the conservative Thai business community, the underlying philosophy surely was one of the key ingredients in the company's success. It was no surprise when he started expanding his operation, taking sea kayaking to Halong Bay in northern Vietnam and Palawan Island in the Philippines, as well as starting Mekong River trips in Laos. Videotapes were marketed, along with a line of tee shirts. The travel industry was booming in Southeast Asia, "eco-tourism" was the catch-phrase of the day, and SeaCanoe made just about everybody's list of peak visitor experiences.

Just four years later, in 1999, John, his company, and the Thai islands on which it was formed were in crisis. Now there were as many as nineteen canoe companies taking up to a thousand visitors a day into the *hongs*; lines formed outside the caves, stalactites were being taken for souvenirs, the noise drove the wildlife away or high into the trees out of sight, and the amount of trash was more than anyone could collect. Most distressing to John, where he said he spent $20,000 a year in training his guides, his competition hardly bothered at all.

These companies also by now formed a Canoe Association and SeaCanoe's membership was cancelled when John went nose-to-nose with a company that paid a million dollars a year to the government for the monopoly rights to collect birds' nests in larger, nearby caves. When a two hundred-baht tariff (about $5) was levied by the birds' nest firm for each canoe passenger, John called it "extortion" and refused to pay. Thereafter, his guides were forbidden to enter the caves by armed men who berated his passengers. At the same time, John started getting death threats and his Thai marketing director was gunned down in the driveway fronting SeaCanoe's offices, leaving him with injuries that kept him on crutches for a year. Pouring salt water into the wounds, the competition asked tourists how safe they thought SeaCanoe trips might be if they couldn't protect their staff. No one was ever arrested and in time, John capitulated and paid the cave entrance fee.

About a year later, the government yanked the nest company's concession, said the area was now a national park and while the two hundred-baht fee remained in place, now it was dedicated to park preservation. "I have no problem with that," John said, "as long as the money is used effectively. However, I see a hundred thousand baht ($2,500) a day collected, but there's been nothing in terms of planning, environmental education and protection. I have no idea where the money's going. Maybe we've just switched from the mafia to the government. It's all the same anyway."

In 2000, John faced his biggest crisis, an employee revolt that squeezed him out of SeaCanoe. They then took full-page ads in the local papers and sent letters by fax to travel agents and repeat customers around the world saying John was out of the business and all future bookings should be made with the guys who took over his company. Where they screwed up was when they signed John's name to the ads and letters. Subsequently, six of his former partners were arrested for libel and when an independent audit was made, their charges that John had embezzled money from the firm were dropped. Impoverished, as he put it, but undaunted, John started another company and paddled back into the caves.

"To say that I am not universally loved is no secret," John once told me. "I'm proud to be an adversary to corruption, deceptive marketing and copyright infringements, tax cheats, copycatting and 'eco-piracy.' I'm the enemy of all dishonest businessmen. This does not endear me to the dishonest folks among us, which leads me to believe that I'm doing my job. I'm sometimes criticized for not fitting in with the Thai way, for going against the grain. But that's exactly why I came here.

"My company brought prosperity to the community," John said. "My rural development scheme brought two billion baht (US$50 million) into Phuket's economy in the last fourteen years. I'm not too happy with the way the other owners have done it, but I'm happy to have provided a livelihood for a thousand to two thousand people. They now call Au Po 'Kayak Harbor', because there are thirty or forty escort boats there. Those boats wouldn't be there if I hadn't come to Thailand."

Fraud Buster

"A young, reasonably affluent Thai couple named Kongsiri immi-grated to the United States, becoming citizens. Life in paradise didn't turn out so well, as it doesn't for many immigrants, so they resorted to the old life insurance scam. They insured the wife and on a return visit to Thailand they faked her death and the U.S. Consulate issued what's called an F-180, The Report of the Death of an American Citizen Abroad. Our embassies and consulates worldwide complete these reports on behalf of the families of U.S. citizens who die overseas.

"The problem is, the Consulate doesn't check authenticity of local death certificates, and just parrots whatever the death cer-tificate says. But bogus death certificates are easy to get almost anywhere. I'll be heading for Haiti next week to handle six death claims, and Haiti is a place where half of my reps have had them-selves declared dead just to show clients how easy it is. I've been declared dead in five different countries."

This is Byron Bales talking. He's an American P.I., a private investigator quite unlike those found in most novels and on TV. He's been visiting Asia for forty years, lived in Bangkok—to be close to the Asian action—from 1990 to 2000, and now he's more or less retired, letting his agency, called First P.I., pretty much run itself, while living in a small seaside town five hours by train from Bangkok.

"Anyhow," he goes on, "the insurance companies paid the claims on Mrs. Kongsiri. She returned to the U.S. sometime later under another name and, of course, another U.S. visa, and continued life with the beneficiary, her husband, in a new place. She was, in effect, both his first and second wife.

"Well, nothing succeeds like success, so a few years later, the husband tried the same trick, having himself die upcountry, here in Thailand. Only this time, there was a snag. Someone saw him in an airport after he was supposed to be dead. One thing led to another and five insurance companies, maybe more, all investigated. Some had already paid the claim, others hadn't. It turned out that, yes, our consulate in Bangkok had handed out another bogus F-180 for the husband. The Kongsiris were caught and extradited to the States."

I met Byron Bales over cans of Budweiser beer at the annual Fourth of July picnic in Bangkok, an all-day event held for American expats on the playing field of one of the city's international schools. Byron said ninety five percent of his work was for insurance companies, chasing down phony death claims.

"There's enough of that to keep you busy here?" I asked.

"Are you kidding? We've had thousands of these cases, all over the world."

And Thailand, no surprise, was one of the fraudsters' favored dying and "reincarnation" locales.

We met during my first or second year in Bangkok, back in the early 1990s, and since then I don't think there's been a week when some runaway criminal or scam artist wasn't apprehended in Thailand, usually in the cities with large expat populations: Bangkok, Chiang Mai, Phuket and, especially, Pattaya, a seaside resort known for its Mafia (Russian as well as local), its bars and at least one foreigner dying violently on average every week.

Thailand regularly is ranked one of the most corrupt countries in the world and in the lawlessness and chaos this encouraged, alongside a tolerant and non-confrontational native population and uncounted thousands of foreign faces on city streets every day, it seemed the perfect place for scammers and fugitives to go unnoticed and unharassed. So long as they kept their head down, likely they could even get away with murder...or in Byron's field, fake one.

A year or so after he and I met, the detective returned to the United States, where he continued to operate an international company with dozens of representatives worldwide. In 2003, we met again in Bangkok after he'd written a novel that was accepted by a local publisher. *The Family Business*, based on true cases, told the story of a brother-sister team who with their parents had other people murdered in Asia to stand in—or, rather, lie down—for them to collect millions in fraudulent insurance cons. We got better acquainted.

Byron told me he was born in St. Louis in 1942 and was from a broken home. He dropped out of school at fifteen and within a year, he was handling "spots" for a local P.I. That meant he was sent to find a target for whom surveillance was requested by a client, then notified his boss of the subject's location.

"Being a kid, no one ever suspected me," he said, "so it was easy work." One day, the detective he was spotting for didn't show up, so he followed the guy all day and was paid $7 instead of the usual $1. Before he was sixteen, he was hiring people to spot for him.

Four years in the pre-Vietnam Marines came next, working for military base security and tracking down deserters. Returning to civilian life, he went to work as a fraud investigator for American Express in New York (picking up overdue credit cards) and then as an underwriting and claims investigator for a large retail credit company. In the evenings he'd sit at the bars in fancy restaurants on his own and when the waiters came by with the customers' credit cards, he'd check them against recent lists and confiscate any bad ones, collecting a $25 bounty for each card, averaging three a night. He also did both criminal bail jumping work and immigration skips—the bring-'em-back-alive work made famous in novels and TV.

"I worked in New York for twenty-five years, from the early 1960s to the late 1980s and it was fabulous. I was involved in politics, did a lot of work for celebrities—the cheapest people in the world, by the way—and I had a fairly high profile in the business, had an office on Broadway and 57th Street. I moved the business out to Long Island, with thirty employees, after we started working international cases and needed space, but didn't need a Manhattan address."

By the time he decided to move to Thailand, he said he'd "worked Europe to death, then Africa, then the Middle East, then Central and South America, and finally Asia. I'd been to over 170 countries and territories time and again. [There are just over 190 member countries in the United Nations.] We'd take a run of cases to various parts of the globe and stay on itinerary anywhere from six to twelve weeks, express mailing completed cases back to New York and wait somewhere for a package of new cases to arrive at the nearest American Express office. That meant we'd ascertain whether the claim was legit or not and send back documentation one way or the other. In time, I decided to live in Asia and handled assignments from Korea to Australia, from Russia all the way across to the Marquesas.

"If we like an assignment and if the money's right, we'll do anything, and we have done everything. But we don't normally work for the U.S. government. They don't pay well and it's usually just too much trouble dealing with them. In fact, the State

Department has been on our shit list for years over all those bogus F-180 documents that they hand out to the scamsters."

Insurance fraud is big business today. Between what are called slip-and-fall artists, swoop-and-squat experts, cappers, Medicaid cheats, flop fakes, accident gangs, unethical doctors, professional whiplash victims, and the Kongsiris and their ilk, the cost to insurance companies is estimated in the hundreds of millions of dollars a year, worldwide. Byron says there's "no way anyone will ever know how hard the insurance industry is hit by fraudulent scams, since so many bad cases are paid because the examiners don't recognize a fraud when it's right up in their face. Especially foreign frauds." He says the willingness of the insurers to settle with the claimants to avoid costly litigation makes them easy targets; the companies matter-of-factly then pass the added expense along to their insured, inflating premiums.

Byron said Thailand didn't have the monopoly on insurance scams. Another favorite destination was the Philippines, with Cambodia, Laos, India, Pakistan, Vietnam and even Burma close behind, though, he added, some of the "nastiest" cases were in the Middle East, where the fraudsters seem quite happy to kill anyone who might be investigating them.

"Runaways are everywhere, and each thinks his hideout of choice is best," Byron says, "—across central Africa, the Caribbean, Southeast Asia, the Pacific, you name it. People have different priorities: hopheads go to Haiti, pedophiles head for Africa and Cambodia, recluses to the Philippines.

"Thailand is attractive because of *mai pen rai* [Thai for "never mind"], it's as simple as that. It's an easy-going culture. They don't care. I've never been to a better country and I don't know anyone who has. The people are great, the weather is great, and the price is right and a long as you don't bother anyone, no one will bother you."

"In Asia, they're fairly easy to break," he said, "and I've handled hundreds where the case was over within six to eight hours after I started. There's a trick to it. It often takes days just to get to these places, but once there, a few simple routines coughs up the truth. One simple method is that we call a MOG, a Man on the Ground. These people are residents who've worked with us for years and understand the business. In many places like the Philippines, we know when a death has been faked. We know who's pushing the claim in the States—the beneficiary, and we know that she knows her husband isn't dead.

"So once we find out where the man is, we send in the MOG dressed as a courier to the village where he's hiding with a courier envelope that's supposed to be from the beneficiary and addressed only to the perp. Only the perp can sign the receipt. The stupid fuck comes down from the hills and does just that. All it takes after that is a camera and a recent newspaper that we hold in front of him and the case is done."

Not all of Byron's business is with insurance companies. He also does what he calls "general P.I. work—locates, surveillances, backgrounds, due diligence, financials. Others are easy as pie. We get inquiries from guys who've been to Thailand, fell in love, and want to make sure their girlfriends are being faithful. We discourage them as much as possible, simply by telling them that if they have doubts, then it's probably the wrong woman for them. We're also very candid. If it's a bar girl, it's very likely she's screwing around on him.

"It's a question of money. Is the guy keeping her up sufficiently? At the beginning of the relationship, the guy was thinking with his wrong head and, having no previous experience, actually thought that after shacking up with the girl for two weeks that he actually meant something to her. Sometimes the client wants an excuse to stop sending money, wants to catch the girl going out with other guys. Needless to say, these are simple cases."

Another easy one, he says, was when a Thai university employee came to him, said her daughter had married "a *farang* piece of shit, and she even lent them money to get started back in the United States. Well, after a few years, she wanted the loan repaid and she started writing to her daughter and son-in-law. The guy got real nasty about it and starts writing her back. Only this peckerhead writes crude messages right on the front of the envelopes which he sends to her at her office. That she's heartless and stingy, yada, yada, yada. It's extremely embarrassing for her, exactly what he intended. The woman came to us. What could we do about it? We investigated the guy and learned that he was on parole. We had a chat with his parole officer and he stopped writing except for an apology. He also paid off the loan.

"There's more. He used postage stamps for his nasty letters. There were some strange looking ones, a few we recognized from many years ago. We had them checked out by a philatelist and learned that, on each of his nasty envelopes the guy had placed stamps worth hundreds of dollars, even though the face value was only the required postage. It turned out the guy had knocked over some old geezer and came away with a fortune in collectible stamps, the value of which he didn't even check. We waited with that information until our client was reimbursed and then let the second shoe fall. I believe the guy is back in the slammer. The guy's bag was victimizing older people."

In 2004, there were more than a hundred private detective agencies in Thailand, employing approximately a thousand private eyes. In Bangkok alone, there were more than forty offices. There were no formal education requirements and, to Byron's dismay, no regulation, although it's a factor he says sometimes works for him.

"Few really know what they're doing and it's like anything else in Thailand: diligence isn't a watchword.

Byron also says that virtually all the private detectives in fiction and film were created by writers who know nothing of their subject. Outside of himself, he says he knows of no real private investigator who's ever actually written a novel and while he doesn't claim to be as good a writer as Raymond Chandler, Arthur Conan Doyle or Sue Grafton, they are the only three in the genre he'd recommend.

The Last Boy Scout

One of George Cooper's closest friends calls him a "truth-seeking missile."

About himself, George says, "There are four things I like more than anything else: women, swimming, beer and taking Cambodian generals to court."

George also says, "I'm addicted to anger," a statement that makes him a perfect fit in Cambodia, where there is a lot to get upset about for a do-gooder lawyer from the United States. In his first four years there, the NGO for whom he worked successfully defended thousands of poor Cambodians who'd had their land confiscated by the military or government, returning their land or winning them compensation; put a soldier in jail for tossing a hand grenade that killed a British expatriate's Cambodian wife; and got three Khmer Rouge bigwigs sentenced to life in prison for giving orders to abduct and execute three foreign backpackers, one of the most high-profile incidents and court cases to come out of the post-Khmer Rouge era.

The obvious question is: why isn't George dead? Why hasn't he had a mysterious car accident during one of his forays upcountry? Why is he being allowed to live and be such a continuing pain in the ass to the Cambodian government? And why is George so determined to antagonize people who have such little regard for rights and life? Does he have a suicide wish?

I met George in 1985 when we lived in Hawaii. He was then in his thirties, one of five children in a family raised in Arlington, Virginia: a Roman Catholic, an avid swimmer whose taut body, close-cropped, wavy hair, translucent blue eyes and rosy cheeks gave him the look of a yuppie. I interviewed him for a newspaper when a book he co-authored revealed long-held secrets about the islands' land ownership and politics. Before that, he worked for tenants and community organizations fighting eviction and environmentally destructive development. In the most high-profile case, defended farmers threatened with eviction when the landowner sold an entire valley to Japanese developers who wanted to replace taro fields and fruit orchards with a golf course and negotiated long-term leases for farms in an adjacent valley. (George won.) After that, he was part of a team that went after an environmental polluter. (And won again.) This, he says now, was "child's play," compared to what he's been doing since arriving in Southeast Asia.

George and I reconnected in Bangkok in 1997 after he took some of the earnings from his last court case in Hawaii and started backpacking around Asia. Since then, during his frequent R&R visits to Bangkok and my visa runs to Phnom Penh, he's become one of my closest friends.

When he first rolled into Bangkok and said he was looking for something "good" to do, I sent him to Father Joe Maier, an American Catholic priest who ran one of the biggest non-profit operations in Bangkok's slums. I figured Joe could use a lawyer who could write and who didn't want to be paid. Not long after that, when George discovered a neighborhood even needier than

Bangkok's Klong Toey slum—Cambodia—he settled there, taking a room no bigger or more lavish than a monk's cell, joined an organization called Legal Aid of Cambodia, a sort of NGO with connections worldwide, and went after "them." It was, for the Cambodians, like have an angry pit bull unleashed.

Before getting into the blow-by-blow nastiness, the nitty-gritty of Southeast Asia at its ugliest, let me say a few words about what George described as "one of the most fucked-up and hopeless countries on earth."

At the time of his arrival, in 1998, the present prime minister, Hun Sen, was sharing the premiership with a son of the king, Prince Norodom Ranariddh, but a year later, Hun Sen, a former officer with the Khmer Rouge, banished the prince in a coup, returning the country to a virtual dictatorship. George said at the time, "Everyone—*everyone*!—in Cambodia has a sad story. Family slaughtered by the Khmer Rouge. Civil war. Decades of poverty. A widespread feeling of hopelessness. There were no exceptions. None."

George's area of expertise was land, so his first assignment was to collect all the existing laws, finding hardly enough to fill one average-sized book. Among his first clients were villagers poisoned by toxic waste imported from Taiwan and two hundred farmers who'd had their land grabbed by an army general. Less than two years on the job, George—who was officially prohibited from working as an attorney in Cambodia and therefore was serving as a "consultant"—along with the LAC represented up to twenty thousand families in land disputes, about forty percent of them involving the military.

If the odds in those statistics weren't intimidating enough, consider what the *Cambodia Daily* called "disorder in the courts." A few of the judges were regarded by George as okay; they'd actually studied some law. But there were many more whose educational records from the Justice Ministry showed considerably less preparation; more than ten percent never finished what is called in the

West "elementary" school and next to some other names the education was termed "not clear."

In addition, the entire country had only two hundred trained lawyers and the Bar Association was making it nearly impossible for more to get certified. Chief among the reasons was that in addition to a bachelor of law degree, new attorneys had to be approved by a center for post-graduate legal training, which was to be "determined by a sub-decree." Nearly six years after these rules were approved, the sub-decree had not been passed. In 2001, the Bar's president said he thought no more than ten people had been admitted (illegally, one is left to surmise) since he took office two-and-a-half years earlier. One of the lucky few was his son. When George showed me the documents and news stories, it occurred to me that George might be one of the reasons for such roadblocks being set up. The government didn't want to risk the chance of any more George Coopers running around with high-minded ideas.

It was into such a judicial environment that this Boy Scout from America rode his white horse, taking a job without pay for LAC until he found sources willing to cover his salary. Four months later, over beers in Bangkok, he told me that he was "seriously committed"—so dedicated, he added, he no longer looked up from his desk at the sound of gunshots, unless they were sustained. Only automatic gunfire now got his attention. And hand grenades that sometimes killed dozens.

In the three years that followed, George came to Bangkok frequently and I visited him in Phnom Penh. Every time, there was a new legal adventure to report. The case involving five thousand land owners who'd been evicted without full compensation when the government widened and realigned a highway, with funding from the Asia Development Bank, came about when George heard they hadn't been compensated, as was required by the government's agreement with the bank. He helped LAC do some studies and went to the ADB. The bank threatened to cut all future funding to the country, and Hun Sen agreed to pay up; then George's assistant got up a plan to start looking for money to hire eight Cambodians to visit all five thousand farmers to see if payment was made. In 2003, the ADB created a plan to figure out what compensation still needed to be paid and offered LAC a contract to help make sure it happened.

In another case, a woman was killed by a hand grenade when a fight erupted between some soldiers and civilians in a karaoke parlor next to the café she operated with her British husband. When the disagreement spilled into the street, she and her husband were closing the cafe's metal doors. Two grenades were thrown by one of the soldiers, one exploded. The woman fell dead. Investigating police found a pistol and thought that could have been the weapon that killed the woman. George had experts from the European Union and the Cambodian police take panels from the door to a firing range and shoot at it with a pistol of identical caliber. Where the breach in the door left by whatever it was that killed the woman was ragged, the gunshots left perfectly round (and much larger) holes. The grenade-throwing soldier went to jail.

Often, George says, it's one piece of evidence that wins a case. That was true when his organization represented the British family of one of three foreign backpackers who'd been kidnapped from a train and then killed. The representation involved three separate cases against three different former Khmer Rouge commanders. In one, when the LAC lawyer and George examined the evidence, they thought that the document that gave the general his alibi had been altered. The general contended he couldn't have ordered the backpackers to be taken hostage, and then executed, because he was in a hospital at the time in Thailand. George thought the document given the court was authentic, but believed the date of his presence in the hospital had been changed from 1995 to 1994.

The British embassy in Bangkok sent the document to the hospital for analysis—something not done by the investigating judge in the case—and in the detailed letter that came back, not only were numerous flaws revealed—making it clear that the document was a total fake—it was pointed out that in 1994, when the general said he was being treated at the hospital, the hospital hadn't yet been built.

"It was like the bomb that went down the smokestack of the *Arizona* at Pearl Harbor," George said, telling the story over beers. "Boom! It just destroyed his alibi." George smiled. "It was great."

Winning court cases wasn't enough for George. Once, when I spent a week with him in Phnom Penh, he introduced me to a waitress at one of the bars frequented by foreigners and told her to smile for me. She did and George said that a year earlier she'd been in a motorcycle accident that killed the driver and removed her front four teeth. "Look at that," he said, her face making it clear that the smile was back. At the same bar, he bought big paper cups of iced soy milk for a dozen or so kids who more or less lived in the parking lot, believing that it might be the only thing worthwhile that they'd had to eat all day. He also bought them clothes and encouraged them to go to school. He was being paid an enormous sum by Cambodian standards now, but at the end of the month, he said he spent some but he gave the rest away.

At the office, he said he was an ogre, but when he was looking for a new assistant, the lines were long, because the previous two had gone to the United States to study on his recommendation. "I tell people, 'It's really hard to work for me.' And that is a fact. Because I just hammer them if they do something stupid. But I think it's really good training. I insist that they produce, and if they do, I'll do everything I can to help." In 2002, his first assistant got her MBA from the University of Mississippi and his second a Fullbright scholarship that led to a BA from the University of Illinois.

"Every candidate for the job expects the same thing now," he said, "—an American education. But that's okay. I wouldn't want an assistant any less qualified. I want someone I can count on, give full responsibility, and know that whatever I've asked will be done, quickly and efficiently. That isn't possible with most Cambodians."

After work, he met with friends, only a couple of them Caucasian. He told me he usually would not socialize with other (Western) NGOs because all they did was talk shop and at the end of the day that was the last thing he wanted. He said he figured that was one of the reasons they burned out so rapidly: it was all they had, or did, or thought, or talked about. Often when he found himself at a table with them, he started to go nuts and soon left. At the end of *his* day, spent pounding on his desk and shouting into the telephone and taking bargirls to the dentist, George said all he wanted to do was party.

Sometimes, that wasn't enough, sending him home to visit his ailing mother or to an island in Greece or the south of Thailand where he stayed alone, did yoga and swam for miles in the ocean every day. His life in Cambodia was withering—in three years his hair had gone gray—and he had to get away.

Much of the time I saw George he was in Bangkok, where, as in Phnom Penh, women flocked to him like bees to honey. But it wasn't his innocence, or his money, that drew them, at least not entirely. The same friend who described George as a "truth-seeking missile" on a visit to Bangkok told me that the secret to getting women to adore George was that he really liked women and listened to them. "Which," George's friend added, "eliminates about ninety five percent of the male population."

When George told me he had given $1,000 to a bargirl he'd met only a few days earlier in Bangkok, as a test to see if she really would quit the business as promised (she didn't), and I reported this act of generosity (foolishness?) to this same friend in

Hawaii, he said that for as long as he'd known George—nearly a quarter of a century—"he has been impulsively and recklessly romantic. This trait, or pathology, gets tangled up with doing good in the world. Sounds like here he goes again: Cooper the serial social-work romantic recidivist. Freud has a phrase for it, as he does for almost everything: repetition compulsion, which operates, as do all things Freudian, powerfully to the point of unstopability, and below the level of rational thought/argument/persuasion."

A final story. A Bangkok bargirl who'd received a letter from one of her French-speaking customers discovered George was literate in French asked him to write a reply for her. For the next hour, he stayed bent over the table, composing, eventually asking for 250 Swiss francs, the same amount the man gave the woman when he returned to Switzerland.

He's happy, I thought as I watched him write. He'd been in Bangkok for almost two weeks and he was finally doing something for someone who was needy and poor.

The Nite Owl

It was my belief that Bernard Trink was not only boring, he was dangerous.

I'd been saying that to my friends for years and I might as well start a story about the man in the same, undiluted fashion. I might also add that by any measure of literature I fear it says a lot about the readership of the *Bangkok Post*, where his weekly column of some thirty years was so popular it reportedly increased the circulation by five thousand copies on the day it appeared, and he lead all other parts of the newspaper's web site for number of overseas hits.

For those unfamiliar with this avuncular American expat, Bernard Trink stitched together bite-sized items in a crazy quilt sort of report from what he called Bangkok's *demimonde*, a French word that means "half-world." He was talking about the bars in Bangkok where young Thai women from the countryside shed their innate shyness along with their clothes and dance in public and then engage in what Trink called "extra-curricular activities" with foreigners, either in their hotels or apartments or in nearby short-time rooms, collecting a negotiated fee.

Some might say Trink was a pimp. He considered himself a journalist and the *Post* regarded him so highly, he was allowed to review films and books. Although he passed his employer's mandatory retirement age, his popularity was regarded so highly that the rule was overlooked, and when he was in his seventies, he was the only freelancer who was, in effect, on a retainer.

Trink's early history was not dissimilar to that of many other longtime expats in Asia. Born in New York City in 1931, he attended classes at City College and Columbia University (according to a small biography published in 2000 by a *Post* reporter, Jennifer Bliss, *But I Don't Give a Hoot*) with an interest in becoming a history professor; Europe between the two world wars was his special interest. He also was an avid chess player and he admitted to not liking either of his parents, but credited them with raising him as a "free thinker."

In 1952, when he was twenty-one, Trink was drafted into the army, serving in Korea and in Japan, a country that ten years later would determine the thrust of his civilian career. Finished fighting and back in the States, he worked as a social worker for a short time and on a European holiday decided not to go home, becoming what Bliss called a "proto-backpacker" for the next seven years, visiting more than thirty countries and arriving in 1962 in Bangkok, where the network of *klongs* (canals) was still intact, American troops had not yet arrived for the Vietnam war, and, as he later put it, "the best girls in Chinatown cost thirty baht [under a dollar by today's exchange rate]." It was while teaching English that he met a Thai woman who was, he told Bliss, "unencumbered by feminist grievances."

Still not ready to settle down, he next worked as a proofreader for the *South China Morning Post* in Hong Kong and in Japan reviewed films for English language newspapers. He also proposed marriage by mail to the Thai woman, marrying her in Japan in 1964, returning to Thailand with her a year later when she was pregnant with the first of their three children. It was then, he said, that he found his first "real" job, as entertainment editor of the daily *Bangkok World*, resurrecting the paper's nightlife column, "Nite Owl."

Initially, he reviewed clubs with foreign entertainers and followed Bob Hope on his annual visits to the American military camps, but soon he added the new go-go bar scene, taking with him a photographer and his own wife, whose respective chores were to take pictures of the dancers and carry the stuff that the club owners gave him. Photographs that weren't fit to publish even in the somewhat sensationalist *World* were pasted on the wall behind his desk, while the more presentable ones were called "The best go-go dancers I saw in Krung Thep this week," illustrating what eventually spread to five pages of stories, gossip, interviews, restaurant and entertainment reviews, and advertisements, giving Trink a substantial share of the newspaper's content.

By 1970, Trink was at his peak, appearing regularly on the radio and with the power of his "Nite Owl" column able to (quoting a colleague at the *World*) "single-handedly determine the fate of a restaurant or a movie by praising or condemning it." To supplement his income, he taught English again, at the AUA and Thammasat University, and film history at Chulalongkorn University.

In 1987, the *World* went out of business and Trink shifted quickly to the *Post*, where he was limited to a single page and was told that he now worked for a "family newspaper," so there'd be no more photographs, nor any of the recommendations of particular masseuses for the "extras" they offered. In time, there were other changes, too, as political correctness swept away his wall of pornography and a no-smoking-in-the-newsroom rule sent him and his pipe to a room for die-hards. In 1996, when his column was cut to half a page, the letters-to-the-editor page was glutted for weeks with curses and praise. As for Trink, he said, "I have no delusions of grandeur, but it's rather like Moses being told to reduce the Ten Commandments to five because he's been given one tablet instead of two." Surely, he was joking.

The most noticeable thing about Trink was his instinct for the banal, because there was so much trivia. Did any of us need to know that he was having trouble finding jockey shorts with a forty-four-inch waist or that the price of Dinty Moore beef stew has gone up again? Could anyone truly care that one of the bars had changed its happy hour policy or was showing football games on a big screen or that there was a mama-san's birthday on Saturday, with a lot of balloons and cold food? This was news? It wasn't even gossip.

Most of Trink's column wasn't even this helpful. More than half was devoted to jokes and the kind of crap you wished people would stop sending to your e-mail address. Of course, this is how he got most of his material; he would not, he said, entertain anything like a phone call in his quest for information. His e-mail address, idontgiveahoot@hotmail.com, echoed the phrase he used to close each column, usually following a long reprint of someone else's alleged humor. Leading this reader to believe he really didn't give one about his readership. Or, maybe had it pegged precisely.

But it wasn't the trivial that bothered me. More important, I thought, Trink's column was obscene. That is, it was about sex, more or less, and it had no socially redeeming qualities. I also regarded it as hazardous to the readership's health. When I went into one of my diatribes with friends or with people I'd just met who might've been faithful readers, there were four points I wanted-ed to make:

   (1) I thought he was a misogynist. He warned newcomers to the Bangkok bar scene (he also made a monthly trip to Pattaya and infrequently mentioned Phuket and Chiang Mai) to beware the bargirls whose only interest was in

acquiring their money by any means possible, and he said marrying one was a sure route to disaster.

Although rip-off stories were common and it was always a good idea to take a prostitute's words with a lick of salt, there *were* many honest bar girls and numerous *farang*-bar-girl marriages lasted many years, some of them indefinitely. Trink's own marriage was approaching the half-century mark, but in the country of his birth the divorce rate was then fifty percent, so his view of a modern relationship's life span obviously was outdated.

Trink's ideas about sex workers changed over time, but never included respect. First, he regarded them as sex objects, then as victims of society, and, finally, as predators who chose an easy but risky way to earn an income that could lead to the bar's equivalent of winning the lottery, finding a foreigner who might provide a monthly allowance and, perhaps, a home and/or marriage. In the meantime, they were paid between five thousand and ten thousand baht a month just for turning up and could pocket a share of the "lady drinks" paid for by customers, along with all earnings from those "extra-curricular activities." Compare that to the five thousand paid to a factory worker or a maid.

"Prostitutes are anything but sweet young things, their smiles covering a hard-as-nails nature," he once wrote. "They didn't choose their profession out of necessity. The vast majority of poverty-stricken girls in the provinces refuse to regard prostitution as an option. Those entering the profession do so because they have the required callousness."

Surely that's true of some, but not all. What struck me as being unfortunate was that I didn't recall ever reading Trink say anything nice about sex workers and their world, and it made me wonder why he chose to spend so much of his time in it. Over the centuries, the arts produced many champions of Trink's "demimondaine"—from Emile Zola and Toulouse Lautrec to John Steinbeck and Jane Fonda—but the Bangkok columnist stood in the opposite corner of the ring, a man with a heart of lead.

(2) More dangerous was Trink's claim that AIDS was absent in the *farang* bars he wrote about. He was wrong! There was a law, I think, that required the women to be tested for sexually transmitted diseases once a week, for HIV every three months. I'd seen some of the girls' cards, with dates and doctors' names stamped in them. Only a few bars enforced this rule and, even then, I wondered how many of the girls merely paid a clinic fifty or a hundred baht instead of the 250 required for actual testing, just to get the stamp.

No matter. The point is, I knew several of the women who died of AIDS, and they worked at Nana Plaza. If the bar owners told Trink the truth, given the number he allegedly talked to and heard about, he'd have reported many more.

(3) Most upsetting was Trink's claim that an HIV-positive diagnosis was unconnected to AIDS. In this regard, he not only denied overwhelming worldwide medical opinion, he sounded like Thabo Mbeki, the president of South Africa who insisted that AIDS was not a problem in his country, despite studies that showed one out of three South African adults was HIV-positive, and according to the United Nations, the average life expectancy in South Africa in 2001 was only forty-seven years, instead of sixty-six, because of AIDS.

Trink endorsed the use of condoms, but I bet his whitewash of the threat in the *farang* bars encouraged many visitors to Thailand to go what was called "bareback" when they got the little ladies (or men) back to their hotel rooms.

(4) Finally, I charged Trink with an abuse of power. That he had lasted so long as a columnist in a daily newspaper, writing about commercial sex was, in that conservative climate and time, almost miraculous, and it was to be applauded. But in the end, he didn't serve prostitution, or women, to the degree he might have. At best, he gave the Thai bargirl a benevolent pat on the head and never any respect or dignity.

Nor had he championed any point of view that might have changed their social position or personal welfare, save to express a wish that bar owners would give them more than two or three days off a month and stop fining them when they arrived for work a few minutes late.

Most abuse of power inflicted its harm through avaricious and even evil acts. Trink's abuse of power was that he had it and didn't use it to help.

In the end, I decided, Trink had to be regarded as a dinosaur. I watched him make his rounds of the bars, his forty-four-inch waistline belted just below his nipples, his Nite Owl medallion around his neck, and every Friday I turned to his column in the *Post* and hoped that this was the one in which he had something valuable to say. Yet, I knew it would not be.

To the powers-that-be at the *Post*, I believed that Trink was an embarrassment, yet far too popular to dismiss. I was wrong. In the final months of 2003, after the Thaksin Shinawatra government introduced what it called a "new social order," Trink was given his walking papers. Effective January 1, 2004, he, along with the long-necked diplodocus and the dodo bird, was extinct, gone, forever, from the notorious Bangkok swamp.

I was, of course, wrong again. In just over a week, his column reappeared on the Internet. He was as important to Bangkok as Wat Arun, he said, immodestly, and there was no killing him off, after all. The column would continue to appear weekly. Just $12 a year.

The Oscar Winner

Stirling Silliphant had lived in Thailand for four years when I asked to interview him for a magazine about his life as an expat, why he'd come to Bangkok, and why he stayed. He agreed and we met, at his request, at the Bangkok Nursing Home, then a collection of one-story cottages where many foreigners went for medical attention. He was there for some tests, he told me, and could see me at noon. The tests were scheduled for that afternoon.

"I came to Thailand to die," he said, simply. He said he'd lived, or worked, as a writer for television and film, just about everywhere, ticking off several of the cities and telling, in amusing and sometimes cynical terms, why he didn't want to spend his final years in those places. "I needed to be surprised," he said. "I wanted to be shocked. Bangkok is unpredictable and it delivers if you give it a chance. Even the small adventures are memorable."

For a man who'd done all he'd done, that was a remarkable statement. At the age of seventy, when he sold his yacht and said goodbye to Hollywood, he truly was someone who'd been everywhere, done everything, and hung out with just about everyone, one of those rare individuals who truly was a legend, a word tossed around promiscuously in Hollywood, yet in his case one that was uncontestable.

Perhaps he was best remembered for his Oscar-winning screenplay for *In the Heat of the Night*, yet during a career that lasted more than fifty years, he wrote or helped write more than two hundred feature films and many more television plays, becoming one of the most important and prolific writers in modern entertainment history. He wrote so much and so fast, in fact, he told friends that he didn't like to show people his resume, because he knew they wouldn't believe it possible.

Born in Detroit and educated in California, he went to work as a publicist for Disney in 1938 and then became an assistant to the president of Twentieth Century Fox before serving as an officer in the Navy in the Pacific during World War II. Returning to the New York office of Fox after the war, he handled publicity for the then-young Marilyn Monroe, returning to Hollywood in the early 1950s after his first novel, *Maracaibo*, became a bestseller. Frustrated by script delays while producing *The Joe Louis Story*, he swore he could do better and started writing for television, generating dozens of scripts for *General Electric Theatre*, *Perry Mason* and *Alfred Hitchock Presents*, going on to write the pilot for *Naked City*, as well as thirty one of its first thirty nine episodes.

In the 1960s, he wrote three-quarters of *Route 66's* 116 episodes and, simultaneously, was the script supervisor for a new, hour-long version of *Naked City* that was nominated for an Emmy in the Outstanding Drama category every year of its run. Years later, he would say that those two series constituted his best work. Production of both shows stopped by 1964, but the "writing machine," as one producer called Stirling in a *Time* magazine profile, didn't slow his pace, freelancing for *Chrysler Theater*, *Mr. Novak* and *Rawhide* and winning his Oscar for *In the Heat of the Night* in 1967. Two years later, he boosted the young Bruce Lee's career by creating a large part for him in *Marlowe*.

He produced *Shaft* in 1970 (and wrote the sequel, *Shaft in Africa*, in 1972), wrote *The Blue Centurions* the same year, and in 1973 helped launch the popular round of disaster movies by scripting *The Poseiden Adventure*, followed by *The Towering Inferno* and *The Swarm*. He also turned his novel about Pearl Harbor, into a television mini-series and wrote Clint Eastwood's third Dirty Harry movie (*The Enforcer*).

A few more features followed in the 1980s, but mainly he comfortably returned to television, writing a succession of made-for-TV movies and two epic mini-series, *Mussolini: the Untold Story* and *Space*, also finding time to publish three adventure novels.

"Silliphant's writing career is remarkable not only for its sheer volume of output, its duration, and its spanning of television and feature work," Mark Alvey wrote for www.museum.tv, "but also for the very fact that he kept an active hand in television after achieving big-screen success, and that, indeed, he considered television to be the medium most conducive to the writer's vision. His Oscar notwithstanding, Silliphant insisted that his *In the Heat of the Night* script was inferior to many of his *Naked City* teleplays. 'As a matter of fact,' he declared to writer William Froug, 'I can think of at least twenty different television scripts I've written which I think are monumental in comparison.' Truth be told, the bulk of Silliphant's features—most of which are adaptations—have tended toward formula, while the passion for character and ideas comes through most strongly in the television work."

With this track record, some were puzzled by what happened to Stirling next, but it wasn't a great mystery. As movie audiences became younger, so, too, did studio executives, who tended to believe that if you wanted to write for teenagers, you had to be only slightly older. By the 1970s and 1980s, "ageism," as it's called, came to roost in Hollywood, building what appeared to be a permanent nest. And where once producers said, "Get me Stirling Silliphant!", now they were calling for "a young Stirling Sillipant."

Before it reached the third, and terminal stage, "Stirling who?", one of the entertainment industry's greatest writers bailed out.

By now, Stirling had a brash and beautiful Vietnamese wife, Tianna, and with her a son, Stirling Jr. The reason they gave for moving to Thailand was to further their study of Buddhism and while that wasn't entirely untrue, it was so stated because Stirling didn't want to burn whatever bridges to power remained in Tinseltown, planning to keep at least one hand on the computer keyboard, while seeing what he could do to enhance Hollywood's connections to Thailand.

In fact, Thailand already had become a popular destination for American filmmakers, building on the success of *The Ugly American*, *The Man With the Golden Gun*, and *The Deerhunter*, filmed there in the 1970s, and subsequently drawing Jean-Claude Van Damme, Steven Seagal, Angelina Jolie, Oliver Stone and many more not just once but repeatedly. *The Killing Fields* was shot in Thailand and so were many of the Vietnam movies (including *Air America*, *Good Morning, Vietnam*, *Uncommon Valor*, *Casualties of War*, *Operation Dumbo Drop* and Stone's *Platoon* and *Between Heaven and Earth*), along with *The Phantom*, *The Beach*, *The Quest*, *Tomorrow Never Dies*, *Mortal Kombat 1 & 2* and John Carpenter's *Vampires 3*.

"He wanted to start a film school and teach a new generation of Thai filmmakers," says Christopher Moore, a Canadian novelist who moved to Thailand soon after Stirling's arrival and who became one of his closest friends. "He also wrote a pilot script for a detective novel set here that he hoped would become a popular TV series that'd do for Thailand what *Hawaii Five-O* and *Magnum P.I.* did for Hawaii."

Chris once told me about the expat life, "It takes an emotional resilience to be on the outside, year after year, required by law to leave the country every three months for a new visa. That may sound like a small thing, but it gives life as an expat a bite, a spin. Concessions must be made. Dreams and desires are changed and shaped."

Not surprisingly, many of these foreign exiles became characters in Chris's novels. "Often they are expats who have shed the skin from one life and created another life. What I find the most fascinating in the characters is their capacity to have re-invented themselves. They ask how do I belong, what do I belong to, and how does this need to belong define who I am, and what am I prepared to risk?

"In Bangkok, with all the freelance expats, it is not difficult to find a crowd of 'unaffiliated' people, searching for ways to survive, to find dignity and self-respect. Such a person is closer to some truth of his time and place than the rest of us, and to follow such a person is to learn some truths about one's self. The character's world and story may not always be pleasant, or politically correct, but it is a truth of our time and our lives."

Surely, Stirling made the same discoveries, so it was not surprising that the hero of this proposed television show was a veteran of the Vietnam war who stayed in Bangkok and "re-invented" himself as a private investigator.

"We pitched Katana [a local production company] and the Thai Farmers Bank for financing," Chris said, "the two of us working together. I remember Stirling taking videos of his films, his Oscar, his novels, his Golden Globe, putting it all on the table. He'd have the whole table filled. We told them all the things we were going to do, the scripts we were going to write, how many hours a day we'd work. They sat there enraptured. We came back four or five days later and they said they weren't interested."

In fact, that pilot film was shot, but *Day of Reckoning*, badly rewritten by its star Fred Dryer, a football player who had starred in television's *Hunter* series, merely became a film shown on TV, gaining—Chris quoted Stirling as saying—the lowest ratings in *NBC Movie of the Week* history.

"For a while, Stirling had a London producer interested in shooting a movie in the Straits of Malacca, where modern day pirates were hijacking everything from freighters full of oil to private yachts. Stirling said we had to put a hurricane in the script," Chris recalled. "I asked why. He said we might get a deal that gave us a percentage of the budget and the special effects budget would be tremendous. I said, 'Let's put in the hurricane!'" Eventually, the deal dissolved.

"Then we did a treatment for a documentary called *The Killing Fields: 20 Years Later*. We got paid for that one, but it never got made," Chris said. The school never happened, either, and every other project Stirling worked on flopped as well.

Chris met Stirling in a Buddhism class and coached him in his Thai, making up a list of the ten commonest phrases that dealt with the heart, the subject of one of Chris's books. "He'd sneak it out in a bar and check it and say, 'Oh, *dee jai!*' He never learned to speak Thai."

I met Stirling my first day after moving to Thailand, in 1993 when he and two young friends took stools next to mine in one of Bangkok's notorious go-go bars. He was stocky and somewhat slope-shouldered and was wearing a lemon yellow sports jacket. He had a gentle face beneath his close-cut white hair and when I heard him and his friends speaking English, I introduced myself. When he said, "I'm Stirling Silliphant," all I could think to say back was, "No shit!"

He laughed and said, "I don't usually get *that* response."

"I know who you are," I went on. "You're a fucking legend."

I had worked in Hollywood, too—experiencing miniscule success—and in the following years we saw each other occasionally, running into each other in a bar or elsewhere with mutual friends, and when I did my interview. He always had something pleasant to say about Thailand and his life, telling me of his discovery of the Chatuchak weekend market, a recent visit to a kick-boxing stadium, or recommending a newly discovered noodle stand. He lived comfortably, in a penthouse when he arrived and then in a succession of roomy houses, where he hosted parties for some of the Hollywood celebrities who came through on holiday or to make films.

There also was a memorable party when he asked several of his expat friends to bring their Thai girlfriends so his could have someone to talk to. (By now, he and Tianna had separated; they never divorced.) The first five minutes, the women chattered amiably, but once it was determined that all came from either different parts of the country or different social classes, and in this fashion sorted out their varying levels of status, none of them exchanged a word the rest of the evening.

"He'd finagle first class tickets to go back to L.A. to fix a script," said Chris. "He'd make a deal: five thousand dollars a day, hotel, car and driver, but every time he returned to Bangkok it was with a renewed conviction that his decision to leave the U.S. was right."

He was seventy-six when I interviewed him at the Bangkok Nursing Home. The tests followed. He didn't say what they were for and I didn't ask. Later, he told friends that he had inoperable prostate cancer. It was two years before I saw him again, when I accompanied Chris to Bangkok General Hospital. The Stirling I had known was a large man, with a full face, thick-waisted. Now he lay in a bed, thin and ill, and so doped up to kill the pain, we weren't sure he even recognized us. After our visit, Chris called his physician and asked how much longer it'd be. The doctor said Stirling already had lived longer than anyone expected.

And more fully, too.

Back when he was churning out scripts for *Route 66*, he received a letter from an eleventh-grader who asked him how he, too, might become a writer. Stirling wrote two single-spaced pages in reply and over the years he and the student became friends. Eventually, David Morrell became a successful novelist, writing *First Blood*, the book that became the first Rambo movie. Stirling helped make another of his novels, *The Brotherhood of the Rose*, into a mini-series for NBC, serving as executive producer.

"Shortly afterward," Morrell wrote, "Stirling told me that in one of his former lives he had lived in Thailand that now he was going home. He had a Beverly Hills garage sale, moved to Bangkok, and had the luxury of writing whatever he wanted, with no deadlines except his own. We often talked about my going there to visit him, but our various schedules kept conflicting. My only contact with him was via frequent faxes. Regret is a terrible emotion. As a little after 8 a.m. on the morning of April 26, 1996...I was eating breakfast, listening to the news on National Public Radio, when the announcer informed me 'Academy Award-winning screenwriter Stirling Silliphant died this morning from prostate cancer. He was seventy-eight'."

Stirling was cremated in a Buddhist temple and a few days later, some of his friends gathered at one of his favorite bars to reminisce. Not then having heard the story about the disastrous party he once hosted, I was the only one who took his Thai girlfriend.

"There was something childlike about him," Chris said, "— something Thai-like. Part of our connection was that Stirling wished he'd come here when he was much younger. In some ways, he almost relived certain aspects of his life here. He lived his missed youth through me. Ageism drove him away from Hollywood. Age doesn't matter that much in Bangkok."

American Pedophile

A little girl appeared on the television screen and was coaxed by an off-camera voice to take her clothes off. She was in a bedroom, presumably somewhere in Bangkok, and wearing an ill-fitting dress. It was difficult to tell how old she was because kids from poor Asian families usually were malnourished, thus small for their age, compared to their Western counterparts. The consensus of the people in the room watching the video was that she was about ten.

The voice was speaking in Thai, but it was clear that it was a *farang* (foreigner), and from the accent an American or a Canadian. Once the girl had been sweet-talked through her shyness and finally was offered a hundred baht, an enormous sum for a child in Thailand though worth less than three American dollars, she took off her dress and with more gentle coaxing, her panties. Now the voice asked her to play with herself.

I was sitting with Father Joe Maier, an American Catholic priest who'd lived and worked with children in the Bangkok slums for more than thirty years, and along with several members of his staff we were watching a videotape the Thai police said was found in the home of Eric Rosser. Joe was told that Rosser, a pianist whose trio backed up some of the finest American blues and jazz singers at the world-praised Oriental Hotel, had been arrested at the request of the FBI after he sent just such a tape to a friend in Indiana. The videotape we watched was given to Father Joe, as he's known, because his organization, the Human Development Foundation (HDF), operated shelters for street kids and Rosser was believed to have found some of his cinematic subjects on street corners.

The HDF's offices were on the ground floor of a run-down four-story building near the port and Bangkok's largest slum. Some of the girls, toddlers up to about sixteen years of age, in the shelter that was located upstairs were sent to Joe by the courts, but others who lived on the streets were free to come and go as they wished, whenever they wanted a hot meal and a safe place to sleep. Police hoped the child might have spent some time in the shelter and that Joe or someone on his staff could identify her, as she stood captured on videotape before us, her little hand between her thin legs, the off-screen voice telling her she was pretty.

The tape, one of many, had been confiscated during a police raid, along with a small amount of marijuana, and Rosser was taken to jail. At this point, it was regarded as a minor story, given limited exposure in the Bangkok press and on TV. Pedophiles in Bangkok? Ho-hum. One of the English language dailies, the *Bangkok Post*, declined to name the hotel for which he worked, protecting one of its regular advertisers. The competing daily, *The Nation*, didn't get any advertising money from the Oriental Hotel, and identified the hotel and bar by name.

Although I'd never had a drink with the man, I knew instantly who he was. I'd written about music for decades and I included the Bamboo Bar on my rounds as it was one of the city's top venues for the blues and jazz. I never met the pianist, but I acknowledged his skill and suggested to friends they go listen to his band.

For reasons not stated by either side, it was to *The Nation* that Rosser then wrote an unsolicited letter from jail that turned his case into one of the biggest stories of the year.

When *The Nation* received Rosser's unsolicited letter from jail, the editors put it on the front page, calling it "The confession of a reluctant pedophile."

"My name is Eric Rosser," he wrote. "Until last Wednesday, I have been known as a gifted pianist and teacher, a ten-year resident of Bangkok with a large circle of friends and colleagues and a wonderful wife and family. I believe my friends would have characterized me as an exceptionally kind, gentle and artistic person.

"Now, since my arrest on Wednesday, I have been exposed as a pedophile. The lurid, misleading and inaccurate stories in the media depict me as a monster of depravity, the center of some sinister pornography ring and serial molester of piano students.

"The reality is more complex, less sensational, and perhaps more pathetic. My life having been effectively destroyed, I have nothing to lose by telling the truth.

"Yes, I am a pedophile. As far as I can tell, I was born this way, or became so even before the age of five. I know the normal sex play of children was an obsession with me. I remained physically immature until I was seventeen. Even when I became an adult, I felt a child within. I still feel this way, a child masquerading in an adult body.

"I have never been able to believe in a God who could have perversely created me this way.

"I have spent most of my adult life fighting rather than giving in to my attraction to young girls. Until I was almost forty, I had only normal sexual relations with adult females, and my desires for young girls have been both fueled and kept in check by an addiction to pornography, the vast majority commercial, adult and available any evening on Silom Road.

"And I have made my own private video tapes. Should the gentlemen who arrested me take the time and trouble to actually wade through the fifty or so tapes I made, they will find hours of film, made in the first years I was here, most of which consists of my encounters with adult prostitutes, chosen for their smallness and sometimes dressed by me as little girls, interspersed with endless telephoto shots of playgrounds, beaches, etc.

"There are only four tapes containing sex acts with immature girls. These represent almost the sum total of my experiences in this direction. Only someone who has experienced a lifetime of frustrating longing could understand what drove me to finally act out some of my fantasies with child prostitutes despite the danger, sordidness and, yes, wrongness. By taping these experiences, I hoped to be able to relive them without continuing to perpetrate these offences. In this I have been successful.

"My sexuality, like my personality, remains essentially childish. There was no force involved in any of these encounters. Even the police, while watching them, remarked on this. I have never had intercourse with a child.

"One of the great current myths about people like me is that we are all involved in large secret societies, in constant communication with one another. For me, and I suspect for most of us out there, it has been entirely the opposite; a long, lonely, secret obsession.

"I have only felt safe enough to reveal myself and trade parts of my collection with two people: one an old friend in the United States to whom I entrusted a copy of one of my tapes, and who gave me copies of his own photographs, and a British man I met while he was traveling through Thailand, who gave me Japanese magazines in exchange for copies of these same photos. I foolishly entrusted him never to sell or disseminate them; a couple of years ago they began showing up on the Internet. I never saw this man again. This is the total of my trading in images. I never sold anything I have made—it was for myself alone.

"Unknown to me, last August my American friend was traced and arrested. My video tape was found, and I was believed to be some kind of big-time child pornographer. On Wednesday morning, the U.S. Police, FBI and Thai Police, trailed by the Thai media, descended on my home. They found instead of a captain of the porn industry only myself, my little terrified family, and my sad collection, testament to a lifetime of furtive longing.

"The most terrible thing about the media representation of me involves the allegations that I preyed on my students. Let me explode another pedophile myth: we are so often called to teaching not out of lust, but from our extraordinary empathy with children. I am a wonderful teacher. The hundreds of students I have taught have passed through my doors unmolested, and I think inspired by my real devotion to their musical development.

"The great media witch-hunt which has demonized pedophiles as the scum of the earth is now reaching epidemic proportions. Turn the statistics of our overwhelming numbers on their head and you have the truth: we are a part of humanity, and have always been so. The genius of creators like Lewis Carroll and Charlie Chaplin involved their child-like approach to the world; they were both pedophiles..."

It's difficult to imagine how Rosser could have thought such a confession might have won him the smallest sympathy. Saying it wasn't a little girl in some photographs, but merely a youthful looking prostitute whom he'd dressed in a child's clothing...claiming there were "only" four videotapes "containing sex acts with little girls"...talking about all the piano students he said he didn't molest...then comparing himself to Carroll and Chaplin must have infuriated readers. Who did this guy think he was?

The response to Rosser's letter was unsurprising, and for nearly three years his case was one of the Thai media's most avidly followed "running" stories.

Two weeks following Eric Rosser's arrest, and with three of the children in the videotapes identified, no one yet had agreed to press charges against the man. After meeting with the mother of one of the girls, a ten-year-old nicknamed Tham, police said they considered her an "unfit guardian" who, in fact, admitted that she had given the child to an older sister to care for five years earlier. The older sister was Rosser's wife and neither she nor Tham's mother would press charges.

On February seventeenth, a special police task force—two officers, two social workers, and an attorney—traveled to Thailand's poor rural northeast to the home of Tham's grandparents to show them a videotape revealing how Rosser enticed her into posing nude for him. At this point, Father Joe's Human Development Centre offered to take custody, traveling to the northeast with the cops six times, an eleven-hour-long journey each way, before gaining cooperation from the child's family. On February twentieth, a group of the girl's relatives, including paternal uncles and aunts, accompanied police to Bangkok, where the grandfather finally agreed to press charges. On March second, the Criminal Court denied bail.

Meanwhile, relatives of some of the other nineteen girls in the videotapes not only refused to take a stand against Rosser, they asked the police to destroy the evidence. When police further talked with the prominent Bangkok families of some of his piano students—who were told that Rosser had rigged video cameras in the toilet and beneath the piano—they, too, refused to cooperate. This was not unusual. Child abuse cases, along with rape, are among the hardest worldwide to prosecute, and in Thailand, especially among the upper class, even the slightest whiff of such scandal would represent a huge loss of face.

Finally, police went to the Rosser apartment, took the girl and delivered her first to the city's social welfare office—where Father Joe said she remained only long enough to become infested with lice—and then was transferred to one of his shelters. The priest's attorney, Chatchai Vongsawat, admitted that it was "very rare for a foreigner to get a jail sentence for this crime [in Thailand], but we are confident that we will succeed this time around. It is an important test case for Thailand and for Thai children who up to now have had no rights in such cases."

Neither Chatchai, nor Father Joe and others at the Human Development Foundation, could have seen what was coming next. Only twenty-four hours later, the child was returned to her mother. The way the law read, if the mother wanted the child, no one else could have her. Thus, with Tham now in her mother's legal custody, the prosecution's case was threatened.

In no way did this development bring lasting comfort to Rosser. Just days later, on March twenty first, Timothy M. Morrison, United States Attorney for the Southern District of Indiana, announced that the forty-eight-year-old pianist, formerly of Bloomington, Indiana, was indicted by a federal grand jury sitting in Indianapolis with six offenses alleging the sexual exploitation of children in Thailand.

"These charges are the result of an investigation conducted by the Federal Bureau of Investigation and the Royal Thai Police," the U.S. Attorney said, "assisted by the U.S. Embassy and the FBI Legal Attaché in Bangkok and the Monroe County Sheriff's Department in Bloomington. The indictment charges Rosser with numerous offenses that include: producing a videotape containing child pornography in Thailand, which includes sexually explicit conduct between himself and an eleven-year-old female child; later distributing that videotape to a Bloomington resident and conspiring to transport, distribute and receive videotapes, photographs and magazines containing child pornography involving female children between the ages of nine and eleven."

It was further said that Rosser faced a maximum possible prison sentence of fifteen years and a fine of up to $250,000 for each count of the indictment alleging conspiracy, distribution and transportation. While the production of child pornography carried a sentence of ten to twenty years and a further fine of $250,000.

At the same time, it was understood that formal extradition would not be requested until after Rosser was tried in Bangkok and, if found guilty, had served his sentence in Thailand. Then on April fifth, Rosser was released on bail.

Police were required to apply to the court for a formal extension of his remand order every twelve days and it was during the latest filing that prosecutors and judges, who said they didn't consider this a major case, bowed to a request from Rosser's attorneys to free him following bail payment of one million baht in cash, equal to about $25,000. In Thailand, that was a lot of money—of sufficient size, it was believed, to prevent the pianist from jumping bail. It also was commonly accepted that a million baht was the "going price" for release from jail for a pedophile.

To Rosser, it must have seemed a bargain. He also must have given thanks to whatever gods he still believed in when police, as was required by law, returned his passport. Rosser then disappeared.

It wasn't the end of the story, though. In the strangest twist of all—after the pianist became the first pedophile to be placed on the FBI's Ten Most Wanted List—Rosser was captured at the Bangkok airport, trying to re-enter the country using a false passport. In the eighteen months he'd been on the run, he had grown a beard and police said he'd had liposuction and plastic surgery to his face while hiding out in the Netherlands, England and France. He said he'd returned to Thailand to visit his wife and child.

This time, Thailand gave Rosser's attorneys no time to maneuver, extraditing him to the U.S., where Justice Department investigators said "a majority of the child pornography involved in the conspiracy was widely distributed on the Internet and is now frequently found in other unrelated cases." Rosser plead guilty in July 2003 to producing, distributing and receiving child pornography and criminal conspiracy. In October, he was sentenced to sixteen years in prison and fined $20,000.

The Odd Couple

If ever there was an odd couple, this one appeared to qualify and, appropriately, their meeting was unusual. Duncan Kilburn was sleeping aboard a plane going from Dubai to Hong Kong in 1993 in business class when he became aware of someone climbing over his seat to get to the vacant one next to his. "Later in the flight," he recalled, "still through a hangover haze, I was aware of him climbing over me again and now as I opened my eyes, I was astonished to see a dwarf hopping from chair arm to chair arm to get to the aisle. When he returned from the loo, we introduced ourselves."

Thus, Duncan, an English saxophone player who was a founding member of a rock band called the Psychedelic Furs before becoming a software specialist with his own company in Hong Kong, met Mark Parr, a onetime circus dwarf from Canada who worked as a programmer analyst for Standard Chartered Bank in Toronto and then for Arab National Bank in Saudi Arabia. At the time of the chance encounter, Mark was on his way to a holiday in China.

Duncan was then a bachelor with a $10,000-a-month Repulse Bay flat, a car, a maid and a Harley Fat Boy, a door prize he won at a New Year's party, and he was thinking about starting a restaurant. Within a year, Mark moved to Hong Kong, and started working from an empty desk in Duncan's offices, which were, he discovered, a fifteen-minute walk to the nearest place where they could get a beer with lunch. That's when they became partners and opened a restaurant and pub that eventually would produce "a small cash mountain" and take them to Cambodia, where they soon lost everything.

I met both men over drinks—Mark in the restaurant and bar they operated in Phnom Penh, Duncan in a Bangkok bar after he'd moved to Thailand to be a house husband while his Vietnamese wife worked as an architect. As is customary in such times and places, we exchanged biographies.

Duncan was born in London in 1955, studied computer science, dropped out, went to work for Reuters, becoming something of a stock and commodity markets specialist, and at twenty-one was posted to New York. He then briefly helped start the post-punk Psychedelic Furs, playing saxophone on its first two albums, remaining with the group for six years, but leaving before its great success in the 1980s and 1990s. By now, Duncan had married and fathered a son. Briefly he worked at the London Stock Exchange and in 1985 he returned to Reuters and separated from his wife. Three years later he was in Hong Kong and four years after that he started his own software company, working for, essentially, Reuters' customers. He says his main claim to fame was writing the software for the blue-and-white ticker tape that crossed the bottom of the screen on CNBC. This is when he met the woman who became his second wife, Nhan, a Vietnamese refugee who had fled to Australia with her family as a child, growing up in Adelaide.

Mark was born a dwarf in 1954, an event that, in his words, "defines your life and can make or break you. My parents brought me up to use my head and not my size [in adulthood, what he calls 'four feet short'], to be an achiever and to have a sense of humor." He, too, was a university dropout, and in 1974 met an

American record producer from Los Angeles who'd once worked as a fire-eater, Barry Friedman, also known as Frazier Mohawk. (Amazingly, Barry was a close friend of mine in the 1960s when we both lived in Los Angeles.) With two others in Toronto, they formed Puck Rent-a-Fool, an enterprise that grew from a clown show to a European-style, one-ring circus that by 1977 had fifty employees, an elephant, and a weekly payroll of $5,000. It toured Canada until it could no longer compete with larger circuses, and its thirty-five trucks were halted by an oil crisis.

That's when, in Mark's words, he and Frazier "ran away from the circus and joined a town, starting our own mini theme park with barnyard animals and circus acts." Puck's Farm opened on fifteen acres half-an-hour north of Toronto in 1981 with a blue-grass band, trapeze artists, a petting zoo, pick-your-own corn and pumpkins, and candy floss; they also kept the elephant and hired out the sides of a small herd of cows for billboards, winning a lot of publicity. They separated after a decade together and in the years following, Mark worked as an actor—appearing in *Equus* with Richard Burton and *Say When* with Charles Durning—and then bought a computer and taught himself DOS, BASIC, Word and Excel. That started his banking career, and in Saudi Arabia, many of his colleagues were from Hong Kong. They inspired his first trips to Asia, which he continued through a one-year contract, earning what he calls "a lot of money." That's when he and Duncan decided to form a partnership.

The Globe, taking its name from the Shakespeare theatre in Stratford-on-Avon, was the first bar/restaurant in Hong Kong's prosperous Hollywood Road area and was an immediate success, getting good reviews and launching the neighborhood as a minia-ture restaurant row. "In our second year," Duncan recalled, "we were literally awash with cash." That was when Duncan and his new wife bought and moved onto a twelve-meter-long sailing boat, where their first son Jesse was born.

Duncan had rowed for years in the Stanley Bay dragon boat races for Reuters and when one of his former teammates bought an old French colonial villa overlooking the Royal Palace and the Tonle Sap River in Phnom Penh, he showed photographs to his friend. "We started to think about what to do with our small cash mountain," Duncan said, and soon went to take a look. Nhan was now working as an architect and she said it needed a full renovation. Mark was dispatched to sign a lease and start the contractors off with $20,000 that he carried in his backpack. Eventually, the job cost ten times that.

Nervous about the impending hand-over of Hong Kong to mainland China, Duncan and Nhan decided to relocate to Phuket in southern Thailand. They set sail in their yacht in April 1997 and three months later Thailand's currency was floated, triggering an Asia-wide economic collapse. The same month, in Phnom Penh, tanks and soldiers took to the streets in a bloody coup engineered by one of the co-premiers who wanted the entire pie. By August, many countries had suspended their foreign aid to Cambodia and Mark believed that "most of our potential customers had left (while) inaccurate news reports of continued violence and crime kept the tourists away."

"We tried everything to boost business—live music, kids' parties, quiz nights and theater," says Mark. Already something of a figure in local theater, Mark began singing with a rock band put together by Duncan, performing on Saturday nights, but nothing seemed to work. "Each time we came up with a new idea, we'd be copied, so we were constantly reinventing ourselves. Menus switched from Asian to European, prices went up and down, and our market fluctuated between the wet and dry seasons, the local expats and the tourists, the good news and the bad."

The Globe in Hong Kong wasn't faring well, either, and the other shareholders voted Duncan and Mark off the board. The staff took over the lease, Duncan and Nhan left their boat moored in Phuket and took a flat in Bangkok—where she worked on one of the city's largest projects, All Seasons Place, and he took daytime responsibility for the kids—and Mark and his new Vietnamese wife, Kim, continued to manage the Globe. That's when I met Mark and when he started coming to Bangkok, to visit his partner and explore the city's nightlife.

I took him to what a mutual friend called an "interactive bar," where the dancers walked around wearing smiles and high heels. Mark was sitting next to me against the wall and opposite the stage, his legs stuck straight out in front of him, when one of the women sat next to him. With coaching from me about the bar's etiquette— "Is this gonna get me in trouble?" he warily asked after buying her a drink; I assured him not—he and the young dancer exchanged the usual Bangkok intimacies. The woman sitting next to me reached across and satisfied her curiosity about Mark, then whispered in my ear, "Sa-mall!" She then fondled me. "Sa-leep!" I said.

Whereupon Mark's new best friend picked him up in her arms like a child and stood triumphantly for a moment near the stage, appearing both amused and amazed by her own bravado. The room erupted with laughter, cheers and applause—reminding Mark, perhaps, of his days as a clown—as she then carried him in her arms to and fro along the length of the bar.

Back in Phnom Penh, business improved as the Globe got mentioned in some tourist guides. "It had been an excellent start to the high season," said Mark, "beginning with the annual water festival in November, followed by Christmas and New Year. The Globe was full of tourists almost every day."

But in 2003, the bottom fell out again when a Thai soap opera actress was erroneously quoted as saying she hoped Thailand would take back Angkor Wat, a world heritage site that was technically a part of Thailand until after World War II. The line actually was no more than something scripted that her character said in the program, and nothing she personally believed, but riots resulted in

Phnom Penh, ending with the Thai embassy and more than a dozen Thai-owned businesses and five-star hotels burned to the ground.

This was followed by war in Iraq and SARS and while there were never any cases of the disease reported in the country, Cambodia generally was a destination tacked onto visits elsewhere in the region, so tourism completely collapsed. "We needed three hundred dollars a day to break even and our takings dropped to less than fifty dollars," Duncan said later. "Some days we took in nothing. The other key issue was that when you fire a staffer in Cambodia caught red-handed with his (or more likely her) hand in the till, they inevitably return later in the day with a half-dozen heavies with AK 47s. Imagine trying to let a dozen staff go.

"We always looked after our staff," he went on. "All were paid on average double the going rate for their jobs. We gave them paid leave and two days a week off, unheard of in Cambodia, and we took more flak from other bar owners over our generosity (actually a misguided attempt to kindle loyalty). They responded by stealing anything they could get their hands on, including Nhan's makeup and clothes.

Duncan and Mark decided to close the restaurant at the Khmer new year (2003), the traditional start of the rainy season. Mark said he paid the salaries up to date, turned off the lights, locked the doors and returned to Canada, while Duncan remained in Bangkok.

"We all went into a collective deep depression," Duncan said, adding that he and his wife had lost $30,000 in the "adventure." He then sold his boat in Phuket for half what it cost him and moved to Australia with his family, where he continued to play house husband, while Mark continued to sleep on Frazier Mohawk's couch.

In early 2004, the two decided to write a screenplay about their adventures, what Duncan described as a "very, very black comedy."

Romancing the Stones

You have to like a guy who openly admits that for years he dealt in smuggled Southeast Asian antiquities, and also is a painter who says his first influence and mentor was a Dutch Boy house paint color chart.

Richard Diran was given that book of paint samples by his father before he could read and write, and it launched the first of his several careers. (I'll get to the stolen Cambodian and Burmese statuary and gold Buddha figures in a minute.) His father likely did that to keep the kid quiet, but Richard says today that he remembers reacting to the colors emotionally; some made him weep with joy, others made him nauseous.

His father was the manager of the Cow Palace, which despite its rustic and somewhat corny name was, during the 1960s, San Francisco's largest auditorium, where the Beatles played their first West Coast concert and the Republicans nominated Barry Goldwater for president (both in 1964). It also was home of the Roller Derby, where Billy Graham held his crusades, Bob Hope told jokes and a 625-pound wrestler named Haystack Calhoun threw his weight around. Richard, then a teenager, had his father's permission to enter the dressing rooms, where he probably made a pain in the ass of himself, if his description of his school days is accurate.

He says he was a "complete freakin' washout" in class, had to repeat the fifth grade, got kicked out of the public school system in the seventh grade for something he says was much more innocuous than things he got away with (which he will not talk about), and then got drummed out of a Catholic school after a priest wouldn't hear his confession because he wasn't a Catholic and Richard told the man to do something anatomically impossible with himself.

The public school system was next, and what he remembers best about his time in it are the summer vacations. For one of these, in 1966 when he was sixteen, without telling their parents, he and a friend, fifteen, planned a trip to the Galapagos Islands; there was one boat a month from Ecuador (then administrating the islands first made famous by Charles Darwin), it dropped you off and picked you up a month later.

"No fuckin' way!' is what our parents said, even though we had our own money," Richard recalls. "So, dig this: when we said we were going anyway, they said they'd give each of us a thousand dollars if we promised not to go any farther than Guatemala. Far fuckin' out, right?"

For two hundred dollars they bought a seven-year-old Ford woody and drove to Mexico City where they met the president of the National Charos Association, who gave them each a pearl-handled, chrome-plated .38 Smith & Wesson pistol and hundreds of rounds in Zapata style ammo belts. No wonder they were stopped by police. Producing the Charos friend's card, they were released and as they continued south, they used the pistols to shoot game, cooking it over a wood fire, using the car antenna as a spit. Despite nearly dying from "something I must've ate," Richard says this trip is what triggered his interest in travel.

Returning to classes, school mates asked them what they did on their summer vacation. "Nobody fuckin' believed it," Richard says, "even when we showed them photographs of the big, weird birds we shot. We showed them the prehistoric human remains we dug up. They still didn't fuckin' believe us." The teachers weren't impressed either, as Richard continued to teeter on the brink of failing nearly everything.

Thank god, he says, for the Dutch Boy color chart, because at art he insists he excelled, next attending an arts and crafts college in Oakland, California, and then, on a full scholarship, joined one of the first classes at the California Institute of Arts, a new school funded by Walt Disney in southern California. He then took the money from the sale of some of his paintings—one went to writer Ray Bradbury—and bought a one-way boat ticket to Japan.

There, on a "cultural visa," he learned Japanese and studied karate. He says his master had never taken a foreign student before and asked if he did so, what would Richard do for him. At the time he had a three-inch-long fingernail that he used when painting as a "dob stick"—the tip of the nail held against the canvas to steady his brush hand, a highly unconventional substitute for the usual wooden stick. Richard said he'd break the nail off. Not such a sacrifice, when you think about it, because it would have had to be removed for karate training anyway, but it was accepted and for four or more hours a day for two and a half years he practiced and in the tournaments always "beat the fuckin' shit out of everybody." (When Richard talks, he sounds a bit like Ozzie Osbourne.) One opponent he says he killed, although he was resuscitated. When Richard tells that story today, he sounds slightly disappointed.

It was also in Kyoto that he met Junko Teramoto a young woman whose hair was green; she was, Richard boasts, "way ahead of her time and way cool." Nothing came of it at the time and Richard returned to San Francisco, where his father got him a job directing traffic in the Cow Palace parking lot, helping move more than five thousand cars around every day and taking the tickets off enough windows and reselling them to pocket an extra hundred or two hundred dollars a day.

However good the money, the job palled, so Richard went back to school, this time to the Gemological Institute of America in Santa Monica, where he became, he says, an expert at gem identification, once again because he was so good with color. And there was Junko again, enrolled in the class behind him. That led to jobs in Los Angeles and San Francisco, the latter with a "truly tortured Jew from eastern Europe" who let him "take gems for a walk," meaning he'd visit jewelry wholesalers with stones that were worth at least $50,000 until he finally unloaded them. He also worked, briefly, for "two criminals" who sent him on his first trips to Thailand to buy gems. Then one Friday, a friend called and told him to take his diploma off the wall of the place and leave, because the Feds were coming on Monday.

It wasn't long after that that he again ran into Junko, who was now planning to open San Francisco's first country-style Japanese restaurant with her mother. Immigration problems soon made it appear she was going to be deported, however, so Richard married her and went to work in the restaurant. And that's where he met two "very, very, very serious boys who were doing Pablo Escobar sized deals," who had read about his prowess buying and selling gems in a newspaper story. He says they gave him $100,000 cash with the agreement that he'd repay them $140,000 in one year, which he did, with enough left over so that the three each had a three-karat ruby as a bonus.

That relationship ended when they sent someone to see him with a necklace to appraise. The guy apparently owed the two gangsters some money and wanted to pay the debt with the jewels. A glance told Richard the stuff was fake and when he called his "partners" and asked what would happen to the guy if he said the jewels were glass.

"We whack him!" one of Richard's partners said.

"Well, it's Sunday and I don't have my tools here, so I can't give you a qualified opinion," he said, "and that," he told me, "was the last time I worked for anybody."

In the ten years the restaurant lasted, Richard continued to make trips to Southeast Asia, working deeper into the jungles in northern Burma, buying gems and jade that he sold when he returned, often to restaurant customers. "You roll a five-karat sapphire across the table to a customer and he goes, 'Woweeeee, lookit that!'

"There was one stone that I bought that was in excess of eight karats, a Burmese star ruby, red like a fire engine with a red star, not a white star, a perfect star with every line equidistant from every other line. Everybody in Thailand and Burma knew about that stone and with the profit Junko and I bought a big house."

Another time, he bought a piece of jade for $500 and sold it for $10,000.

Just before the big earthquake of 1989, the restaurant was sold and for the next three years he remained in the Bay Area but also had a house in Rangoon. This was soon after the Burmese generals refused to recognize Aung San Suu Kyi's victory at the polls and put her under house arrest and the country under martial law with a curfew of nine p.m. "We had a fuckin' sound system with a Chinese amplifier and Chinese speakers that we ran off a fuckin' Walkman, you could hear Motorhead three fuckin' blocks away," Richard remembers. "The neighbors complained, SLORC sent some guys over, I gave them a bottle of Black Label and told them to tell the neighbors to fuck off. We had parties, man, half a dozen beautiful Burmese girls, sometimes friends visiting Burma, other times local friends, nine o'clock, nobody could go home, so everybody'd pair off, I had six bedrooms, martial law and the curfew. It was beauuuuuutiful!"

This was also when he was dealing in what are called "antiquities," the ancient artwork looted from some of the finest temples in Burma and Cambodia. "I was buying it, I was selling it," Richard admits. "We had caches of solid gold Buddhas, man! I was selling to museums all over the world. What capped it for me was I had a very important tenth century piece and it wound up at Sotheby's for auction and some professor of Burmese studies at the University of Chicago recognized it and went to the FBI. It may have been the only time the FBI worked with the Burmese government to try to prosecute an American citizen: me. What they said, essentially, was, 'Give it back.' I said, 'Take it,' and I got out of the antiquities business."

He was still traveling back and forth to San Francisco during this time, but the long commute was getting tedious and both he and Junko agreed with something Mark Twain said about the coldest winter he ever experienced was a summer in San Francisco, so in 1991 they leased their big house with the view of the Pacific and moved to Bangkok, where they've remained ever since. Why Bangkok?

"I spoke some Thai"—he is now fluent, and knows some Burmese and Shan as well, on top of the Japanese and high school Spanish—"and it seemed this was the land of the free, people here didn't seem interested in doing anything if there wasn't *sanuk* involved. If something wasn't fun doing, hey, don't do it. That's my style. And, even in Bangkok it's rural enough you can get a chunk of land right in the middle of town that's big enough to have your chickens, your dogs and your exotic animals."

Richard wasn't kidding. Before we left the bar where he's a regular at Bangkok's Washington Square, a neighborhood known for its fermenting expats, many of them left over from the war in Vietnam, he called Junko and told her to "lock up all the dogs!" He said she had fourteen. The chaos that greeted us when we arrived in what is regarded as a quiet, upscale neighborhood seemed appropriate for Bangkok, however improbable, because in Thailand you come to expect the unexpected. The four full-time employees (not counting the maid) were building new shelters for the hundred-plus fighting chickens. The leopard cubs were sleeping, but an eagle with the size and charm of a pit bull was angrily banging away inside one of those cages you ship dogs in when traveling on a plane. (Junko has four eagles, Richard added–two more than the Bangkok zoo.) Junko, with fresh lipstick and cold Heineken to greet her guest, stood near where we sat, smiling enigmatically, an island of calm, seeming a true descendant of both geisha and samurai, as Richard insisted she was.

"This is what Junko likes doing here, and she's good at it, she's real good at it," said Richard. "There are no other Japanese doing cockfighting in Thailand, and there are no Thai women doing it either. It's not brutal like in the Philippines, in Indonesia, even in the United States. There's no sword on the back of the foot, the actual talon is taped up, it's like chicken boxing, and she's good at it, man. All these Chinese mafioso have taken her under their wing and taught her very well about breeding the best fighting chickens.

"We only have one neighbor who can hear us, they hate us and we hate them, but he's a civil servant, he can't do shit. I mean, the cops are coming to our house every two days to buy chickens! So if the neighbors want to complain, we tell them in really rude terms, 'Fuuuuuuuk YOUUUUUUU!'"

The trips to northern Burma continued, despite the ongoing skirmishes between some of the ethnic minorities and the military government and the "drug war" being waged between the Wa army and Thai border forces, some of whom were among the Wa's best wholesale customers. For a while, Richard's business wasn't affected. He'd raise his right hand on entering Burma from Thailand and say, "I'm free of political taint," and he'd get his visa.

It changed when the Wa switched from heroin to amphetamines, which were easier and cheaper to produce and from the 1990s onward, the Thai population's drug of choice. Where before, the producer-smugglers were merely filthy rich, now they were making so much money they had to find ways to hide it. Suddenly, the supply of "important stones" dried up. They still were being dug out of the soil, but now, Richard said, a $100,000 stone was not offered to him but would go instead to the Wa, who'd pay twice that and then claim they resold it for $300,000 and then pay taxes on the $300,000. In this way, he said, nearly a third of a million dirty dollars got "washed." A generation ago, he said, they were chopping off heads with swords from horseback and now they were into international finance–had university-trained chemists from China running the laboratories and invest-ment bankers on their payroll in Switzerland.

Richard returned to art. The oil painting stopped many years before and to take its place, Richard bought a camera and start-ed photographing the colorful hill tribes he encountered during his search for gems and jade. He did this for sixteen years, com-pleting his documentation after he was one of the first visitors allowed into Nagaland, a remote area of Burma near the India border. In 1997, Weidenfeld and Nicolson in London published a hefty "coffee table" book of his pictures, *The Vanishing Hill Tribes of Burma*, in time for the United Nations' decade of the World's Indigenous Peoples, and it became a bestseller. He also began painting again, big surrealist canvasses with mythological, violent and/or erotic themes.

"The ninth painting in the series is of the Cyclops stuffing one warrior into his mouth, biting off his head," Richard told me. "In his other hand he is squishing another guy while five other war-riors with swords and shields raised look on in shock. It's lots of fun painting the expressions on the bastards' faces. My model for the Cyclops is an Englishman who is just fucking huge, not mus-cle-bound, just huge. Ex-special forces guy who is in charge of Shell Oil security all over the world. Does a thousand pushups a day. Great model. Fifty-two years old, so has the bursting veins in his shaved head so necessary in a Cyclops. I had him grip a mango in one fist while tearing into another one with his teeth. These mangoes are the warriors. He was surprisingly shy about posing for me. But he did it, man! Standing out there in the alley behind the bar. It was quite cool."

Back at the bar around the corner from the room where he hangs the finished paintings, he waved his arm and said of his fellow drinkers, "Mostly it's guys who're at least as old as I am"–he was born in 1949–"and most have served in the military and were in the CIA and you have guys who were mentally wounded, or physically, or both. Most seem to have developed some sort of life for themselves now. But they're also outlaws. Like me. They're outside the law, outside American law. I think all of us realize we don't fit there anymore. When I go back to the States, I know I look like everybody else, but my brain doesn't fit any more.

"And they're interesting, man. There's more interesting people you can meet in Bangkok in one day than you could meet in a lifetime in Los Angeles and LA's filled with interesting people, you just never see them. In Bangkok, everybody's out on the street. The stories you hear from people here, elsewhere you'd say, 'Man, this guy's totally full of horseshit,' but here it turns out to be true. Which is not to say you don't have the liars and shills and shysters, but you meet a more diverse group of people here.

"As for the *farang* women, forget it. For a *farang* woman, unless they got something to do, they're really up against the fuckin' wall, they're bored to death. They know there's no way they can be as lovely and feminine, with the soft skin and wrinkle-free and no bumps on their ass as ten-million girls you're looking at every day. They can't stack up to that, they get washed up real fast. Let's face it, it's a man's town.

"I have very little in common with anybody in the States. They've got it down to a science, you never make enough to get off the treadmill, paying off the house, paying for the kids' shoes, paying your wife's alimony, whatever the fuck it is, you're on the treadmill for the rest of your life. It's perfect. It's beautiful. If I were going to create a system of slaves, that would be it.

"Yeah, man, I'm a lifer. I'm not going back. I'm going to be cremated here, I'm going up the [crematorium] chimney."

Richard had just returned from Burma, where he visited a young girl in Rangoon who was born without the bottom of one leg beneath the knee and for whom he'd bought a prosthesis. That was when she was twelve and now she was fifteen and it didn't fit any more. As he told me her story, the obscenity fell away. He said that the girl's upper leg had withered and she was in rehabilitation for twenty months to build it up before the first device was fitted. When she outgrew it, her mother didn't call Richard and he didn't think about it and now she had to go through the same process again, but Richard said he felt she could do it. She had a strong will and, sure enough, after another eight weeks of rehabilitation, mom was complaining in a lovely way that the girl was mobile and riding her bike again; before, Richard says, her sister had to give her a lift to school. Of course, in another couple of years she'll need still another prosthesis. This time, Richard said he was going to stay in touch.

"I mean, like what else can I fuckin' do?"

He was quiet for a moment as he stubbed out his umpteenth cigarette and sipped his umpteenth Scotch on ice, and asked, "So who else am I going to be with in this fuckin' book of yours?"

"Oh, a Catholic priest and a couple of Vietnam spooks, some bar owners, a few writers, some whores and a pedophile, people like that."

He laughed and said, "Fuuuuck YOUUUUUUU!"

Two days later he left for Burma to fill up a suitcase the size of a king-sized bed with monkey skull Naga artifacts for resale to a trader in the United States.

Mr. Cool

He slides onto the barstool next to me, granny glasses perched atop his shaved, graying head, a small ring in his left earlobe, his wispy jazz goatee moving as his husky New York voice pours forth...and if I didn't already know he poured the best drinks by the fastest and most knowledgeable staff in town, he told me again, weaving the message into another great story about running a bar in Bangkok.

There are many who say David Jacobson runs the number one bar in Asia. For more than a decade, his Q Bar, first in Saigon and now in Bangkok, has been named one of the ten best in the world by numerous magazines as well as the suppliers of the booze he sells. When the history of bars is written, he may not get an entire chapter, but he and his upmarket saloon should get more than a footnote. In Southeast Asia, the Q Man is Mr. Cool and his saloon is the Thai capital's hippest up-market joint to see and be seen and to dance, while ordering from the largest selection of labels in the region.

The son of a Jewish corporate lawyer and a midwestern— WASP department store buyer in Manhattan, he believed in "the Beach Boys' California dream," so he attended a California university (majoring in political science) and after working for the Bobby Kennedy presidential campaign that ended with the candidate's assassination, disillusioned—"all my heroes were being killed"—he turned to photography, shooting Dustin Hoffman, Mel Gibson and Tom Cruise, among others, doing publicity and posters for the Hollywood studios. This was in the 1970s and 1980s. He'd always wanted to see Southeast Asia, and after photographing a former *Playboy* centerfold who was the wife of a man employed by a charity in Vietnam and Cambodia, David told the man he'd take pictures of his operation for free in exchange for travel expenses.

In 1990, David's friend took actor Ed Asner to Southeast Asia and asked David to document the trip. David was then dating Nguyen Phuong Anh, the daughter of refugees who escaped from Vietnam in 1978, settling in Pasadena. A sister drowned during the escape and her parents remained ferociously anti-communist, so when David asked her to accompany him, she was forbidden to go. She went anyway and went to work for the charity. At the same time, David decided he'd hit the ceiling as a photographer in Hollywood because he didn't play the game; there was, he said, a lot of "babysitting" when shooting the stars.

His first trip to Vietnam, he traveled as a journalist and was limited in his movement. On a second journey a year later, as a tourist, he saw more of the country and noticed that "all these people from all over the world were coming in, panning for gold in the government's new market economy. I decided to 'sell pans.' Everybody was going to need a place to drink. There were no good bars in Saigon. I decided to open one." The long, shallow space David found in the National Theater seemed ideal. It was right smack in the middle of town, equidistant from the Continental and Caravelle Hotels. Several restaurants had failed in that location. So, fronted by Vietnamese partners, his plans were given little attention by the People's Committee, the city's government body that was busy dealing with international oil companies and the likes of Proctor & Gamble.

Thus he opened, in 1993, without fanfare. A little over two years later, on the twentieth anniversary of the fall or the liberation of Saigon—depending on your point of view—the world's journalists who covered the war returned in a pack. They, too, needed a place to drink and when they met the beautiful Anh—a Viet *kieu*, a returning boat person, who now hosted Saigon's most successful bar—everyone filed a story. Thus while David remained in the background, the joint's quiet "manager," the Q Bar went onto the map.

In the years that followed, the government hassled David, introducing a rule that said foreign liquors could not be sold, but allowed him to sell his current inventory. David agreed, sneaking into the bar in the middle of the night to refill the bottles. Next, the tourism authorities approached him and said they'd take care of any problems that might arise in exchange for fifty one percent of his business. He said he'd close the bar first and after a month or so, for some reason they backed off and the rule about foreign booze was reversed. Meanwhile, the Q Bar went onto the cover of the *New York Times Sunday Magazine* and was the subject of a week of *Doonesbury* cartoons.

"Matt Dillon was hanging out right away," David recalls. "He introduced the bar to Robert DeNiro. John Kennedy Jr. came in with Daryl Hannah. Kate Moss was coming in with Bruce Weber. I took Norman Mailer and his wife around the city. They all wanted to see Vietnam and came to us because we had the best bar. We had the only place in Saigon where there was sidewalk seating. The motorbikes drove past as people table-hopped. It was like *La Dolce Vita*."

The bubble began to leak air in 1997 when the Asian economy collapsed and David's best evenings were the going away parties for companies that, simultaneously, got fed up with the strangling corruption and red tape. In 1998, the government refused to renew David's visa, wouldn't even let him back into the country to clean out his apartment. Some said it was because he took photos of Saigon slum housing for the *New York Times*. (He had asked that he not be credited for the pictures, but his name appeared in print anyway.) Others said the People's Committee was embarrassed to have an American running the city's most popular bar and a government-operated tourism business opened a joint nearby and didn't want the competition. Some even said he was with the CIA. For a year, he waited in Thailand, during which time he and his girlfriend separated and the bar closed. That's when he decided to re-open in Bangkok.

All his friends said he'd fail when he leased a 1960s Thai house at the end of a remote *soi*, then spent a small fortune remodeling it and said there wouldn't be any "working girls" in the place. There were other challenges. For what he paid his entire staff in Saigon he now could hire *one* waitress and he had to charge less for the drinks. In addition, while it took him a month to train staff in Vietnam—teach everyone the two hundred basic words (straw, ashtray, Scotch) and learn everything they had to know about Western drinks—it took a full six months in Thailand. The Viets also worked harder and were better educated and anxious to please. The Thais didn't match these standards, but while the Vietnamese never trusted anyone—not even their parents and surely not another employee—which made for little camaraderie, the Thais came together like family. They worked better as a team, they genuinely liked each other and became friends, partied together after hours, moved in with each other. Five years after opening, some of the original employees were still on staff, almost unheard of in the bar business.

The cops were always a problem. In Saigon, they didn't understand why anyone came to the bar, because there was no TV, no karaoke, no drugs, no take-away girls. But in Saigon, David says, there was only one police force, whereas in Thailand there were the national cops and tourist police and immigration authorities, on and on, and the faces kept changing and every new one had conflicting rules to play by.

Unlike the Saigon police, Thai police hung out in his bar, a factor not comforting to his regular customers. And when the new prime minister launched a "new social order" campaign, they started raiding his bar, locking everyone inside until they'd been tested for drugs, leading them one by one into the toilet to pee in a cup with a cop in attendance and then had them wait until a police "chemist" tested for amphetamines and Ecstacy, two of urban Thailand's most popular drugs; it happened one night to me and my son when we visited the bar.

Another story: David's new girlfriend, Phuong Kim Tran, also Vietnamese, had work papers allowing her to serve as the bar's manager and when a cop found her behind the cash register, he threatened to arrest her because, he said, she wasn't a cashier. Once again, David was playing a chess game with authority.

Despite all this, the new bar was another success, initially attracting all the Thai "hi-so," or high society, a fickle bunch that moved on, leaving David with a core of dedicated Thai and foreign drinkers attracted by the drink variety—forty different vodkas in a freezer, an equal number of single malt and blended Scotch whiskeys, bourbons, tequilas and after dinner drinks—fast service, and the newest music, selected by four staff DJs along with a regular sprinkling of imported ones.

"We poured bigger drinks," David says. "We decided rather than try to get thirty pours out of a bottle, we'd get fifteen and charge a little more, not double, and make stronger drinks. The *farangs* loved it and so did the Thais who'd been educated in the West, a significant part of our customer base. Some of the Thai women complained, so we put a warning on our menu that said we poured 'New York measure.'"

When David and Phuong were married, they invited all their friends to a reception at the bar and arrived themselves in a Rolls Royce led by a Thai marching band playing John Philip Sousa. While the music at the party was jazz, opening with Frank Sinatra's "You Make Me Feel So Young." He slid onto a barstool next to me that night and said of the song then playing on the sound system, "Listen to this. Betty Carter. I saw her in New York and Sarah Vaughan was in the audience."

Sitting at the top of the heap—again winning "Best Bar" awards from the time he opened—David became an expert on Bangkok's bar scene and their customers. The go-go bar scene was for older guys who wanted to get laid, not drink, and they drank beer, so he wasn't interested in them. The English and Irish pubs were somewhat more efficiently operated but offered more beer and sports on TV. Both of these scenes played "music from their generation—'Hotel California' and Santana—and were aging," he said.

The gay scene was more interesting—with better music and a spirited Thai-*farang* mix—as was the backpackers' Khao San Road, which was fast going upscale, and drew another lively mix of locals and foreigners.

At the same time, the "big Thai scene" offered five thousand capacity discotheques, deafening techno music, beer and whisky, and the staff didn't speak a word of English. Smaller, more exclusive Thai bars catered to spoiled Thai brats in a lounge setting, serving kamikazes, black label and beer.

None of it was of much interest to Mr. Q.

The Q Bar was the future, David said. The music was cutting edge—lots of house and hip-hop, no techno—sometimes with live performers—a violinist, a trumpet player, a percussionist, an *avant garde* vocalist—playing or singing on top of the DJ's tracks. The customers were approximately half-and-half Thai/*farang*, with more Thais on the weekends (they had less money, so could drink less frequently), more foreigners mid-week, coming from all over the world. Lots of Indians, who owned much of the property in the neighborhood. Concierges and food and beverage managers and chefs from the five-star hotels who weren't permitted to drink in their own hotels on their days off and didn't want to go to the competition and wanted good service and drinks; David says some brought their staff with them "to show them how it's done." Foreign entertainers playing Bangkok came on their night off.

The bar was and wasn't a pickup joint. "Working girls" were discouraged by the five-dollar cover charge (which covered two free drinks once inside) and by the fact that most male customers were there to party, not find a date. David also refused to give the girls the lockers for their clothing and purses that were customary in some of the other upscale bars, including some in five-star hotels.

On the other hand, he said, "The bar was designed to get people to move around. It's dimly lit, so you can only see from certain angles and if you're attracted to someone and you can only see him or her in silhouette, you have to get up and walk around. We put the bathrooms in the back, so everyone has to walk the length of the bar. To go upstairs, where there's another bar and a big outdoor patio, you have to walk around the bar and across the dance floor. That way, people socialize. See what people look like, what people are wearing. We don't have a TV. We want people to talk to each other. I can understand a bunch of guys in a sports bar watching a football game together, but that's not us. I can watch TV at home. I want to look at attractive people, meet interesting people."

I met David at the original Q Bar in Saigon shortly after it opened and we've been friends since, and I've now let him toot his own horn. That said, I think it's a horn worth tooting. He's a classy guy who lives the sort of life many expats and would-be expats can only fantasize about. He's doing precisely what he wants to do, and he enjoys trying to talk you into joining him in his fantasy.

He was forty-five when he moved to Saigon in 1992 and opened the first Q Bar—with just three hundred dollars left to his name when he opened—and he was fifty-one when the Vietnamese said go away and he started all over again in Bangkok. Now he has what is arguably one of the best bars in the Asia, his home is tastefully packed with Southeast Asian art and antiques, providing a quiet refuge at the end of a gardened *cul de sac*, and he's married to a young woman who, as I wrote this, made him a daddy for the first time at age fifty-six.

He still takes photographs, but nowadays they're snapshots of his wife and kid.

Green Thumb

When Bill Warren moved to Bangkok from the United States in 1960, the road on which he lived, today called Rama IV for the fourth king in the Chakri dynasty, had canals running down both sides. Now there are no canals and a highway fly-over throws a forbidding, dark shadow down the middle and you can hardly see Lumpini Park across the street for all the noisy traffic and bad air. But in 1960, water buffalo–then Thailand's only source of "beef"–were herded down the road at night from the train station to the slaughterhouse, a distance of several kilometers.

One night, one of the beasts wandered into Bill's garden, where he found it in the morning, contentedly eating his flowers. Bill sounded the alarm and instructed his gardener, Sawai, to send the buffalo on its way to become the Thai equivalent of T-bone and porterhouse. The teenaged Sawai protested and found someone with a truck who took the buffalo to a farm in his home village, where the animal lived to an old age.

Today, Bill has another garden in a less trafficked part of Bangkok, where Sawai still toils, forty-two years later, "but now as the manager of my household," his employer says–and Bill's earnings from three separate but interlocking careers sent Sawai's children to private schools. Bill retired from teaching, the first of his professions, in 1990 after thirty years as a lecturer at Chulalongkorn University, named for Rama V. A second career he insists is only a hobby, but the gardens he has designed complement some of the finest hotels, homes and public buildings in Thailand and have led to the writing of numerous books about tropical gardens and plants.

It is this last career, writing, for which he is best known. With the publication of forty-eight books over three decades, as he became known as "the dean of Thailand's expat writers." He has offered foreigners and many Thais what has come to be recognized as the first and best look at much of Thai culture and history. Besides the gardening books, he has written five about Jim Thompson, the founder of Thailand's modern silk industry, who disappeared mysteriously in 1967; two more about the Chao Phrya River; the text of a massive volume that accompanied pictures by fifty photographers, *Seven Days in the Kingdom*; four about Bangkok; more guidebooks than he wishes to remember (he once wrote an article titled "Why I'll Never Write a Guidebook Again"); a history of aviation in Thailand; centenary books for the Siam Society and the Royal Bangkok Sports Club; large format volumes about traditional Thai arts and crafts, Thai cooking, Thai architecture, Oriental cooking, the Grand Palace, His Majesty the King Bhumibol Adulyadej's fifty years on the throne, Thailand's "heritage" and "treasured" homes, spirit houses and elephants, to compose a partial list. No other writer in Thailand, either Thai or *farang*, comes even close.

What makes this feat all the more remarkable is that approximately half of the books remain in print and many are in the $40-50 range. Bill says he is proud to have seen two of them, *The Tropical Garden*, which includes gardens in Thailand, Indonesia, Singapore and Hawaii, and the best-selling *Thai Style*, in the offices of many

Asian architects, "who copy a chair, a screen, a lamp, a path, a roof line, a swimming pool. The books have had a sort of life and influence I never expected." Thus, he is not only the most prolific foreign author in Thailand, but arguably its most authoritative.

"I have a wicked friend who says my books are about my friends' houses," he said over drinks on his verandah at the end of his work day, his way of seeing friends without having to venture into Bangkok traffic. "It's not true, but there is an element of the truth in it. Because you have to know the homes if you are to write about them intelligently."

It's also advisable for an author to have a passion about his subjects. Even after more than four decades in Bangkok, Bill insists he remains as entranced by the city as he was when he first read a story—while still living in the United States—by a writer who saw a tram car that struck a pedicab, which in turn rammed into a taxi, causing the cab to swerve and fall into a canal on top of a boat selling charcoal. Bill so likes this anecdote he tells it in three of his books, saying, "I knew then and there that I just had to live in a place where such things happen." It is, he contends, this "same general air of unpredictability, of chaos just around the corner," the city's "messy, carefree way" that, once here, convinced him to stay.

It was also, he told me over a genteel whisky and water at the end of an afternoon, a place where foreigners were given the fertile environment in which they could re-invent themselves. Jim Thompson, a former World War II spy, became identified as the individual most responsible for creating a worldwide market for Thai silk. Anna Leonowens, best known for the largely fictitious memoirs that eventually became a Broadway musical and Hollywood film, *The King and I*, was another re-creation—one whose fabrications were revealed by Bill in an essay that gave one of his story collections its name. Thailand's history was strewn with, and defined by, such people, Bill said. The phenomenon started in the seventeenth century, when a Greek named Constantine Phaulkon became an extremely influential figure in the court of King Narai. And so it has been ever since.

On the other hand, Bill has not so much re-invented as found himself in Thailand. Born in 1930, he spent a sheltered childhood in the American South, entering Emory University in Atlanta as a "sixteen-year-old virgin when all the returning war veterans were enrolling at age twenty-eight on the GI Bill, having been shot at and having their lives destroyed by war for five years. Once a week I was supposed to call my godmother, Margaret Mitchell [author of *Gone With the Wind*, a lifelong friend of his mother's]. I did that, dutifully, but I also grew up fast." With a university degree in journalism and short periods of employment at the *New Yorker* and CBS Television in New York behind him, he traveled to Manila to work with a documentary filmmaker. That job sent him to Bangkok in 1959 to do a film about Jim Thompson that never was finished. However, he became friends with Thompson and his chief assistant, Charles Sheffield, with whom he shared a home after deciding he'd live in Bangkok. His first books, about Thompson's home and antique collection—today a popular tourist attraction—and a biography of Thompson, were published in the late 1960s and dedicated to Sheffield, who died in 1973.

Other books followed as regularly as troops passing in review, as Bill filled in the intervals by writing for many airline magazines, *Reader's Digest, Gourmet, Esquire, Architectural Digest,* the *International Herald Tribune,* and the *New York Times.* Except for the guidebooks—which he says were written for money and "because I was afraid to say no when asked, fearing no one would ever ask again"—the books were created when he saw a need.

"There were no books about Jim Thompson and his landmark home. There were books about Thai jewelry, Thai silver, Thai ceramics, and so on, but no single book that brought all the Thai arts and crafts together. *Thai Style* was the first to look at traditional Thai houses. When an old friend sent me a collection of slides he'd made of spirit houses, I thought it was a subject for a magazine article, not a book, but then I realized that there were no books about the many kinds of what I call 'spiritual abodes.' Some, like the Erawan Shrine, have Indian influences; others are more Chinese and those with four supporting poles and a ladder are thought to be linked to the earth while those with one pole are connected to the sky.

"As with so many things Thai," he adds, "of course there is great disagreement about everything."

He tells a story about a singular shrine on the grounds of what is now the Nai Lert Park Hotel that was lost in weeds at the end of a shady lane behind the British Embassy. This was more than forty years ago, when Bill moved into a house on the property, alongside the Saen Saep Canal and adjacent to "a dense mini-jungle" that offended him for aesthetic reasons and the fact that it was inhabited by snakes. When he asked his landlady if he could clear it, she said there was an old shrine on the property, home of a female spirit called Chao Mae Tuptim. Removing the waist-high grass, he discovered that the shrine comprised of phallic images, some of them several meters in length. Now it, too, is a site sought out by visitors as well as worshippers.

"When I came here," Bill said, "there wasn't even a history of Thailand in English and there were no other *farang* writers. For a long time, I had the field to myself. Everything was just waiting to be discovered."

He had another advantage. He calls it "luck," and perhaps that's what it is, but from the day of his arrival, he had the entré that his friendship with Jim Thompson offered. This took him into Bangkok's highest social echelons. One connection led him to the next and to all he took the gracious manner associated with the old American South. Like many Thais, there was little Bill liked more than gossip, but he never shared it with others; discretion and the trust it engendered was as important to him as the devotion to accuracy he learned from the "fact-checkers" at the *New Yorker* and *New York Times* who nit-picked his stories into final shape. So it was no surprise when Prem Tinsulanonda, prime minister through most of the 1980s and, later, the president of the privy council, asked Bill to write his authorized biography. And when the Royal Household wanted a book about the Grand Palace to use as a gift for visiting dignitaries, Bill was asked to write it, too.

Bill also credits three friends for their help: Pimsai Amranand, who "taught me everything I know about tropical gardening" [her son Ping later provided photographs for several of his books]; Darrell Berrigan, founder of the now extinct *Bangkok World* who "let me write a column on gardening in his weekly magazine in the early '60s"; and Princess Chumbhot of Nakorn Sawan, whom he describes as "probably Bangkok's most famous hostess, with whom I lunched almost every week for more than twenty years. All, alas, are now dead, like almost everybody I knew in my early years here."

Such associations might lead to rampant ego, or at least aloofness, in others, but Bill is steadfastly reserved. He seems truly amazed that *Thai Style* has sold more than a hundred thousand copies and that *The Tropical Garden* has been translated into twenty languages—insisting that he contributes little more than something to accompany beautiful photographs. (He has worked with thirteen different photographers, most often with Luca Invernizzi Tettoni, a flamboyant Italian photographer with whom he has collaborated nineteen times.) He almost shudders when people call him an "expert." For example, he has no great love for Thai food, although he wrote one of the most attractive and praising expositions, *Thailand the Beautiful Cookbook*, a volume that weighs almost as much as a small sack of rice, with sales (mainly in the U.S.) also surpassing the hundred thousand mark.

About this book, Bill says that without his approval, his publisher described him in a press release as "the world's foremost authority on Thai food." When his servants saw the story in a Thai newspaper, he says, "they rolled around the floor in laughter, then taped the story to the kitchen wall. I am not a cook and never said I was. All of the recipes in the book came from a professional chef, who is credited. What I like to write about is the culture from which the cuisine was created."

Even about gardening, the author sounds unusually hesitant. As a child, he says, he had no interest in the subject and whenever he planted something, it died. Once emigrating to Thailand where, he discovered, the geography and climate welcomed even the palest green thumb, he added flowering plants and trees to his list of passions. Soon he began to design gardens and, of course, write books about them. Today his work can be seen at the Phuket Yacht Club, Meridian Phuket Hotel, Jim Thompson House, U.S. Embassy Residence, and the ESCAP Building in Bangkok, and in 2004 he renovated his original design for the old Hilton Hotel (now the Nai Lert Park Hotel), what Bill says is "the largest hotel garden in Bangkok and perhaps in all of Thailand."

Bill is now in his seventies and, in his words, "what Eudora Welty once described as 'underfoot locally,' with the established commitments and routine activities that felicitous phrase implies." He only does "jungly gardens," not caring for the carefully arranged ones fancied by many Asians. Yet, his own life is disciplined, as orderly as a manicured hedge. Except for the room where he writes. It looks as if a bomb went off in a paper factory. "When I go out of town, Sawai stacks everything up," Bill said, "and it takes me weeks to find anything."

He writes every day, seven days a week—"even if it's only one or two pages"—and as the afternoon light in his own garden fades, he settles his bulk into a comfortable chair with a pack of cigarettes, alone or with friends, and sips drinks brought by his loyal friend Sawai.

He's a big man with the thinning gray hair cut short and brushed back. ("No pictures!" he said when I approached him for this book.) His benign smile and the soft Southern accent of his youth lend a gentleness to his tales. His knowledge of Thai culture and history is great and his contacts extend deep; one friend says, "What I wouldn't give to have a copy of his Rolidex!" Yet at small dinner parties at his home, to which it is a privilege to be asked, the gossip—served with what almost invariably is western food—discreetly concerns characters who've been dead for half a century.

One time, he recalled seeing a photograph of what appeared to be a woman hanging on the wall of the palace of Rama VI, a monarch during the early twentieth century known for adding to Siamese literature a wholly new genre, the spoken, Western-style play. Often he performed in some of the dramas he translated and sponsored publicly. The "woman" in the photograph, Bill announced to the startled palace attendant accompanying him, was none other than His Majesty himself.

Much of his information comes from local libraries and his own collection of "a couple of hundred books dealing with the subjects I write about," including about fifty on tropical botany. He also has a Thai researcher with contacts that run deeper than his own, who also can find her way in the National Archives, and "someone good at the computer. I'm not very adept searching the Internet."

Nor, he insisted, has he welcomed other modern conveniences. "I started out with no gadgetry when I came here," he said, "and I gave in, one by one. I had no gas, no hot water, no air conditioning, no telephone. We wrote a note: can you come to dinner tonight? Jim Thompson never had a telephone at home. It didn't seem necessary." Does he now have a cell phone? "No!" he exclaimed, "And I'll never get one, either." How about a web site? "Why would I want one? I'm not selling anything," said the man with more than twenty books in print.

Bill is a legal resident of Thailand today—"the least the Thais could do for me after I taught for the government for thirty years," he says. It is a rare moment of immodesty, accompanied by a chuckle without bitterness. Bill considers himself, first and last, a scholar, a student of his adopted home, regarding the pupil-teacher relationship as the one that defines the heft and thrust of his life.

"I'm constantly running into my former students," he says. "They've done well since they escaped my lectures. I'm proudest of the women, who could only go on to teaching careers thirty years ago. Now they are in top positions in advertising, public relations, tourism, and business.

"It makes life a little easier for me. When I enter an office, I discover someone who remembers me, for some unimaginable reason, and they want to help. The Thai have a respectful regard for their teachers and I don't discourage that. Look what Thailand has taught me, after all."

Been There, Done That

When it comes to chest hair, few in Thailand's testosterone-fueled expat community can come close to a man who said he was a "sissy" as a child growing up on a farm in the United States. This is Harold Stephens, arguably one of Asia's most remarkable adventure travelers, a man once told by James Clavell, author of *Tai-pan* and *Shogun*, that were he to write a modern saga, he would base it on his life.

Steve, as he is known to friends, sat next to me in Singapore when we met, at a dinner hosted by Hans Hoefer, the founder/owner of the much-praised *Insight Guides*. (For whom Steve had written some books.) At the time, I had no idea who Steve was, but when, a few years later, I moved to Thailand, I was told that in all of modern Asia, as well as much of the rest of the world, no one could, or would, ever push himself harder to create an adventurous life and reputation.

He was a U.S. marine in the Second World War who was imprisoned by Chinese communists, and escaped by swimming to a passing junk in the dead of winter. He built a seventy-one-foot long schooner, taught himself to navigate by the stars, and sailed around the Pacific for eighteen years, barely surviving encounters with ferocious storms and marauding pirates, finally losing the ship in a hurricane off the coast of Hawaii. He dove to the wreck of HMS *Repulse* in the South China Sea, took a camel caravan across Afghanistan, trekked rain forests in Southeast Asia looking for lost cities, floated down the Amazon on a raft, rode ponies into the Himalayas, climbed the Matterhorn and most of the major peaks in North America, and even briefly joined forces with one of Sir Edmund Hillary's climbing teams. He spent a month in the Malaysian jungles counting elephants and looking for white rhinos. He drove a motorcycle across Australia and a Toyota land cruiser around most of the world, getting arrested twice during India's war with what was then called East Pakistan, now Bangladesh, putting more than forty two thousand miles on the odometer.

Serendipity brought even more glamor in a Forrest-Gumpish way: being in the right place at the right time. A classmate of his, and the only woman enrolled at Georgetown University at the time was named Jacqueline, wife of the junior senator from Massachusetts, John Kennedy. And while living on Tahiti he was an extra in MGM's production of *Mutiny on the Bounty*, befriended Marlon Brando and kept secret for forty years the existence of two Tahitian children fathered by the star; the kids still call him Uncle Steve.

He also happened to know a woman who was Burt Lancaster's mistress and when his first book was published, he gave her a copy. She passed it on to the actor when Steve was visiting and he dismissed it, saying, "I guess people will read anything nowadays." Steve came right back with, "Same thing with the movies. People will go see anyone in a film today." Lancaster laughed and they became good friends.

"I knew many celebrities," Steve recalls, "and, like with Brando, I never wrote about them, so they trusted me. A big New

York editor at Random House offered a hefty advance when he saw my journals, but when I said I'd have to cut some of the stuff about Brando, that was the end of that."

Just as many adventurers before him, it was all fodder for his uncounted (he says they number in the thousands) articles and an uncertain number of sincerely-and-simply-told, up-close-and-personal books. How many, exactly? "Maybe twenty four," he says, "but that includes *A Motoring Guide to Malaysia and Singapore* that I did for Shell Oil. Is that a book?"

There's no question about his biggest seller—forty thousand copies—*At Home in Asia*, a collection, like this one, of profiles of expatriates. In it, he wrote of himself and his friends as searching for the "rainbow's end." What is it that makes someone want to be an expatriate? "It's not the lack of love for one's own country, or from the desire to flee from an unhappy home," he wrote. "Nor is it for political, economic or social reasons. The motives are deeper, and more complex. The answers to why the people in this book have become 'expats' I leave to you to discover for yourself as you read about their extraordinary lives. But keep in mind, these people were not born into the lives they lead; they created them."

So, too, Harold Stephens. Reading his stories, it's clear that this was a man not merely influenced but also obsessed by the same shelf of writers who inspired so many others to leave home, audaciously—Joseph Conrad, Jack London and Ernest Hemingway, among the more obvious. Eerily, in early photographs, Steve is a dead ringer for the young, mustachioed Hemingway; even today, the resemblance is startling if you take away novelist's trademark beard and leave the gray hair and mustache.

It all began unremarkably, as the son of immigrant parents in western Pennsylvania—his mom a Hungarian, his dad a Russian (named Stepanovich upon entering the U.S. as a child). Until he was eleven, life was spent on his father's hundred-acre working farm.

When the farmhouse burned to the ground, dad went into the coal mines and after school every day, Steve followed him, working the four o'clock shift. The family's financial needs soon made him choose between the two and the ninth grade was his last.

No loss, really, he says today, because he was the one the schoolyard bullies used as a punching bag and he was always the last kid chosen in sandlot games. Steve's size makes this hard to believe; shaking hands with him today is like putting your hand into a catcher's mitt. What happened? It was reminiscent of an advertisement appearing in all the magazines at the time, showing how a ninety-seven-pound weakling who got sand kicked in his face on the beach became a hulking brute.

Instead of signing up for one of Charles Atlas's mail order body-building courses, a week before his seventeenth birthday, in 1944, Steve enlisted in the Marines. Three months later he was in Okinawa, part of the Second World War's largest land-sea-air engagement, a battle that took the lives of 23,000 Americans, 91,000 Japanese and 150,000 Okinawan civilians. The war soon ended and considering his prospects—a return to the mines or work in a steel factory—he re-enlisted and was sent not home but to China to assist in repatriating Japanese troops back to Japan.

It was in China that the young Marine discovered mystery and intrigue. Crates and crates of prehistoric human bones, representing the only such collection on earth, dating back to the Peking Man, disappeared in the post-war chaos. As did a fortune in gold looted by the Japanese. As did the descendants of White Russians who had lived in China since the fall of the last czar and after the war were sent back to Russia. No one yet knows what happened to the bones, the gold or the Russians, although it's fairly certain that Stalin had a welcoming committee waiting for the royalist returnees.

Steve further experienced his first great adventure in China (overlooking for the moment Okinawa), when after four years in China and being arrested by Mao Tse Tung's Red Army, no friend of the U.S. military, he escaped by swimming two kilometers through icy waters to a passing junk.

It was his next assignment he says proved to offer a "reawakening." That came when he was trained as a member of the elite First Marine Guards, a unit sent to U.S. embassies as bodyguards to the ambassadors, but also to "snoop" (his word) on embassy employees. "We'd look at typewriter ribbons to see if the ones used to type classified documents had been locked up according to regulations, that sort of thing," he recalls. His first assignment sent him to the embassy in Paris, where he remained for two years, drinking in some of the same bars as Ernest Hemingway.

One day, Steve recalls, the ambassador asked him if he liked his job. Steve said he was proud to serve as the man's bodyguard. "Bullshit!" said the diplomat. "Wouldn't you rather be me?" He then explained that all Steve needed was an education, so with the Marine's consent, the ambassador got him appointed to Georgetown University, and Steve left the military after eight years.

While still in Paris, a Philadelphia society girl (from a social circle that included Grace Kelly) married him to spite her parents and, once back in the U.S., she had two children by him. When Georgetown learned he didn't have a high school diploma, he was expelled. He took a hurry-up course to get one, was readmitted and following another accelerated agenda he earned a Bachelor of Science degree in foreign service in two-and-a-half years—hello Jackie, bye-bye Jackie—and then, still believing he wanted to follow in the ambassador's footsteps he spent three years at the National Security Agency and took America's foreign service exam. It was in vain. He knew he'd never be able to toe the political line and in 1959, when he and his wife divorced, Steve did what many men might have done in such a situation: he took his folder of unpublished short stories and went to live in Tahiti, leaving his kids with his ex-wife.

Because he had to leave French Polynesia every six months for a visa, Steve continued traveling, hitching rides on copra boats and flying, when he had the money, to Asia. He started selling stories to an American men's magazine that paid $2,500 for each of his two-fisted articles. "Two of those and I could live for a year," he says. By 1966, he had moved to Thailand and was working fulltime as a journalist, first for the English language *Bangkok World* and then for the *Bangkok Post*.

This is when the *serious* travel began. With Thai Inter-national Airways as a sponsor and the *Post* a ready market for his stories, Steve started living out of a duffel bag, motoring around the world and writing his first book, *Who Needs a Road?* In 1971, he built his schooner and then wrote countless stories and a book called *The Last Voyage*. The boat was called The Third Sea. Why? "Surely you know about the Third Sea," Steve told people who asked and all nodded yes, of course. "It didn't mean a damned thing," Steve says. "When someone asked Jack London why he named his boat the Snark, he said he couldn't think of anything else."

It was at the *Post* where he met his current wife, another staff writer, Michelle, a Thai-Filipina who had three young sons from a previous marriage. In 1986, Steve moved his family to a farm surrounded by redwood trees in northern California, so his boys, aged five, six and seven, could get a western education and "learn carpentry and how to pour cement and how seeds turned into vegetables." Between visits to California—up to six round trips per year—and while keeping a flat in Bangkok, or living aboard his boat, anchored at the mouth of the Chao Phrya River, more books followed, their titles reflecting his muscular restlessness: *Discover the Orient, Asian Adventure, Turn South at the Equator, Wander with the Wind, Singapore After Dark*. In this fashion, he adhered to a tradition that reached back centuries, turning the old Roman cliché *Vini, vidi, vici* ("I went, I saw, I conquered") into "I went, I saw, I wrote."

"Every time I saw a mountain, I wanted to climb it," he says. "Way back in the 1950s at a party I heard someone say something about the Matterhorn. I said, 'What's a Matterhorn?' When I found out, I climbed it."

Obviously you cannot sail a seventy-one-foot long schooner comfortably without some help, and he admits to having company on several of his journeys or at least for parts of them, giving credit to his nephew Robert Stedman for being not only his No. 1 supporter over the years but also his best friend. Robert was twenty-one years old when Steve says he "quit school, his job, ditched his live-in girl, and to the horror of all my family, my mother included, he joined me in Honolulu. Tahiti was fine, but it was a tough trip across the Pacific. We ran into a full typhoon, but made it to a small island in the southern Philippines. Fearing that the typhoon was making a loop and returning, nearly all the crew jumped ship. With Robert and two others, we went back out to sea and then lost the winds. Had no fuel and little food. We were adrift for seventy two days, with the current carrying us deep into Indonesia, and sure enough, we were hit by pirates. We escaped in the black of night. The next day we met them with loaded guns and they let us go."

Steve insists, however, that most of his adventures were solo ones. "If you wait for others," he says, "you'll never get it done."

The same attitude has directed the recent path of his literary career, putting an assortment of Bangkok, Singapore and Hong Kong publishers behind him to start with a lawyer friend, in 1992, a company called Wolfenden. (Again, the name means nothing, is made up from "random syllables.") So now he self-publishes, a growing trend internationally. Some people sniff at this, but many big names, including Mark Twain, did it. For Steve, what it means is that the number of books sold may be smaller, depending on the author's distribution, marketing and promotion skills, but instead of earning a royalty of six to maybe fifteen percent of the cover price, now he realizes as much as seventy five percent.

This, along with a continuing contract with Thai International to produce in-house periodicals and stories promoting the airline, along with freelance sales to a slew of regional magazines, allowed Steve and his wife to move in 2004 into a compound in a quiet, upscale neighborhood in Bangkok that has two houses (twelve bedrooms!), separate servants' quarters and grounds so large there are full-time gardeners.

"I asked the lady who owns the property how much she wanted for it and she said three hundred million baht ($7.5 million)," Steve says almost apologetically. "So I asked her why she's renting it to us for so little. She said it was an old Thai house and Thais with money today want modern, so empty places like this are available." The rent? About the same as a small, two-bedroom condo in an area like Sathorn or Sukhumvit, but still more than the author can afford, so the second house will be subleased.

It was decades following his split from his first wife before he saw their kids again. Steve says everything is good between them now. The daughter is a great success, a retired stock broker with houses in Boston, on the beach in California and in Spain. The son joined his dad on The Third Sea and under Steve's tutelage learned to navigate by the stars, but decided he was a landlubber at heart, and now has a cattle ranch in California.

His three adopted sons moved back to Thailand when Steve and their mother did and together they now operate a company with thirty employees that creates advertising on-line, the sort of messages that show up on Steve's computer that he says he "hates." Two of the times we met to talk for this story, one of his grandchildren was present. Domesticity has come to sit on his lap.

This doesn't mean, at age seventy-five, that the sissy turned adventurer is taking up golf. Steve still works out in a gym with weights, looks at least ten years younger than he is, and he continues to pack more travel into a month than most people do in several years. Much of this is done on the cheap, or free. "Asia is very much a barter society," he says. "Somewhere else, you pay cash for your travel. Here, you go to an airline or a travel company with a story idea and they give you tickets and hotel rooms. So I stay on the road." The week I finished writing this profile, he was off to India to begin a cross-Asia journey, tracing the Buddha's "footsteps."

With his nephew, Steve's also planning to build another boat, this one to explore Asia's largest rivers, and there is a book he's been working on for years about "the Asian woman" that he knows will cause western feminists to foam at the mouth.

"I'm a dinosaur," he said, "and I'm proud of it. When I was sailing my schooner, I did it all with a sextant and a stopwatch, following the stars. People said, 'Why don't you get modern navigation equipment? It'd be so much easier.' Well, there's more to sailing than getting from A to B. When you're navigating the way I do, you become conscious of the universe and how we all fit into it."

So, You Want to Own a Bar in Bangkok?

Steve Watson and Steve Bird, known as Big Steve and Small Steve for their vastly contrasting physiognomy, were two of the Vietnam vets who ran the Three Roses Bar in Bangkok's Nana Plaza. Like many bar "owners" in Thailand, the two Steves and a third pilot, who perhaps wisely remained in Africa where he continued to fly choppers, bought the bar following decades in the bars as customers.

At Nana Plaza, a majority of such businesses were managed by foreigners, mainly Europeans and Americans, who also provided the initial investment, but legally the majority owners had to be Thai, so the Three Roses was in the name of Small Steve's Thai wife. Once they paid the "tea money," a non-refundable sum paid the lease-holder for a sub-lease, the rest was easy. The new managers met with the police and negotiated a monthly "fee" based on the size of the place and the number of dancers and whether they'd dance topless or not or if there'd be a "short-time room" in the back of the bar, and etc. They then remodeled, called the liquor distributor, explained the rules to the staff, announced an opening date, and were ready to embrace wealth and bliss.

The two Steves decided from the start that they wouldn't run their place like some of the other bars, where the girls were treated like cattle. There was one bar manager who made new employees buy two pair of overpriced dancing boots from him, while owners of some of the larger, more popular places insisted the girls have twenty or more "buy-outs" a month. When customers paid a "bar fine" of 350-500 baht (up to $12) to take the girl to a short-time room in the neighborhood or back to his hotel room or apartment—for which he additionally negotiated a price for the woman's services—it was explained that the fine covered the lost drinks that would've been purchased for her by other customers if she'd remained on the premises. The truth was, bar fines were expected to cover her salary. Fines levied for tardiness, absenteeism or failing to rack up the requisite number of bar fines often resulted in an empty pay envelope at the end of the month. In addition, the girls customarily were given only three days off a month, and no allowances were made for illness or trouble at home. On several occasions, I paid my girlfriend Lamyai's bar fine so she could go see her kids.

Even the Steves went along with some of the rules, paying their girls less than the bigger downstairs establishments while requiring eight bar fines a month. One of the things that made them different was how generous they were with leave time. Some called them suckers, but they trusted their instincts when a girl said one of her children was sick or there was some other family problem. If they believed her, they gave her time off, kept her on the payroll and didn't fine her for her absence. When Lamyai's father was sick and subsequently died, they gave her time off and kept her on salary, just as they did when I was hospitalized for surgery and she spent three weeks with me. How their employees felt about them was evident each year on Valentine's Day, when the dancers and hostesses piled the Steves with gifts.

As time passed, the girls came and went; turnover in such a

business was regular and expected. Besides those who married, others got bored and quit. Two died of AIDS. And slowly the percentage of girls with Cambodian heritage fell, until you couldn't call it a Khmer bar any more. Day-to-day management of the girls typically was left to the mamasan, Noon, a sad-eyed thirty-something whose husband had left her with two children to support. She seemed to run a tight ship and was trusted, as was the cashier, Ple. When I was in the hospital, Noon came to visit twice.

Steve told me that sometimes there was a profit, but it was never large and during the off-season he and his partners dipped into their savings and the two Steves regularly took turns flying choppers for a commercial outfit in Indonesia to cover the deficit. Tourism was booming in Thailand, even after the region's 1997 economic collapse, yet as the visitor numbers went up, so did the number of new bars, leaving everyone with a thinner slice of the customer pie. When the two Steves sub-leased Three Roses, it was one of sixteen bars in the Plaza. Five years later, there more more than forty and another dozen new ones in the immediate neighborhood.

Drink prices were kept low at Three Roses, going against the decision to raise the cost of a beer by as much as fifty percent by two other managers, who together controlled nearly a third of the bars in the plaza. Three Roses tried harder. Tee-shirts and baseball caps reflecting the helicopter motif of the bar were sold at fair prices. The two Steves hung a public phone on the bar's outside wall using the bar number, and the cash generated from their employees and passers-by paid for one girl's salary. Buy two Carlsberg drafts, and you got the third one free. Still, sometimes it was as late as the twenty-eighth of the month before they had enough in the bank to meet the next month's payroll and rent.

I always sat at the outside bar to watch the human parade, talking with the Steves, who usually sat there, too. I learned that Big Steve's last tour in Vietnam ended when his chopper took a rocket and crashed, and he was thrown through the windshield and found still strapped to his seat a hundred meters away, his face hanging in shreds. He didn't seem to mind when I told him that as he was mending in a hospital, I was marching in the streets in Los Angeles, protesting the war. In fact, when he finished reading Robert McNamara's book in which he confessed that he really opposed the war when he was LBJ's defense secretary but didn't say so, both Steve and I cussed him and clinked our beer bottles in a toast to his future ill health. "If that sonofabitch didn't want me there, he shouldn't have sent me," Steve said. The two Steves and I became friends.

There were, generally, three types of bar at Nana Plaza, defined by their location. On the ground floor were the larger, flashier places, some that had more than a hundred women on the payroll. These were the most popular with the tourist trade. The second floor, where Three Roses was located, was characterized by smaller, funkier bars, many of which depended on a steady stream of *farang* residents like me. While the third floor was known for its crude sex shows, staged mainly because as any shopping mall operator will tell you, it's difficult to get customers to the upper levels. (And why most of the malls in Thailand put restaurants or movie theaters on the top floor.)

One of the regulars at Three Roses described it as being run more like a club than a business. Three Roses was one of numerous bars that catered to a hard-core expat clientele, without whom, Big Steve once told me, the bar would likely die. Thus the joint became my "local," where I drank with friends whether or not Lamyai was in town.

So I was disappointed when I learned that Noon, the mamasan, had been stealing between $1,000 and $2,000 a month. By the time it was discovered, she had a condo, a motorcyle, an unknown amount of cash in the bank and plastic surgery to make her eyes look less sad (a failure, I'm happy to say), and when they fired her, she took about $700 from the cash register along with the ATM card and cleared out the last $2,000 in the account.

"She stole indiscriminantly," Small Steve told me. "She took liquor, tee-shirts, hats, anything she could carry."

How had they finally discovered what was going on? More interesting is the question: why were they so blind? Big Steve was present every night, but he sat outside getting tanked on beer, apparently oblivious. I was told that everyone in the bar knew what was going on, but they remained silent. Thais didn't tell *farangs* when other Thais were ripping them off and, besides that, Thais were non-confrontational and they surely didn't want to get involved in someone else's problem. Unless they had a grudge and wanted revenge. Which is what happened at Three Roses. It was girls Noon had fired who snitched.

A couple of days later the two Steves posted a notice on the outside wall by the phone (in English and Thai) saying Noon and the cashier Ple were dismissed for "misconduct." Small Steve told me he was going to press charges. But he didn't really expect to get much joy. It wasn't their country, after all.

It was an old story. Surely it'd happened in many bars before and would occur in many more. I wouldn't have minded it happening to the guy who sold boots to his new employees at inflated prices. Or another Nana Plaza bar owner who sold quarter shares in his place to eleven *farang* investors. It bothered me when the good guys got hit. For the chopper pilots it was a bigger disappointment, of course, turning what they thought was a wet dream come true into a topless bar where they lost their shirts.

It was only a week or so later that I met a young man at Nana Plaza, who'd been in Bangkok for just a few months. He said he was enamored of the city and its carnal opportunity and asked me, "Can you give me a good reason for not opening a bar here?"

"Yeah," I said. "Tell me first, do you like bars?"

"Are you kidding? I love them!"

"If you want to change that and end up hating bars, own one. That'll do it."

I elaborated for about five minutes, telling the guy how it wasn't a way to get rich or meet women but instead was a constant hassle putting up with your employees' drug and alcohol and gambling habits and failure to come to work; what do you do when you have twenty five females on the payroll and only four show up? Can you ever be sure the girls aren't drinking your whisky and the cashier isn't helping herself to the cash? And you won't ever own the bar, because it has to be in a Thai's name, so what if your Thai partner decides he doesn't want you around any more? The police will drive you nuts, too. And then the air conditioning system will die during the slow season, when your cash flow is running in the negative. Think about your customer base, I said: men, drinking.

"No," he interrupted. "Men getting laid."

"Wrong. Men getting laid happens after they leave your bar. So long as they're in your bar, they're men getting drunk."

"Yeah, but I don't hear much about violence."

"How about general assholery? Only a few get violent, but most of the others you wouldn't want to meet even if they were sober, and when they're drunk every one of them thinks he's your new best friend, or wants to tell you how to run your bar, so he's going to talk to you and you'll listen, because you don't want to lose him as a customer. Think of it as a lifestyle wrapped in lies, boredom and debt, peopled by men and women you probably wouldn't otherwise want to know, let alone spend every night of your life with. Seven days a week, two days off a year when the bars close for the Buddha's and the King's birthdays. If you don't drink too much now, you will."

In time, Noon was replaced with a male "manager" who seemed to be both honest and efficient and a few months later Big Steve died suddenly (but unsurprisingly) of liver failure. A sign was posted outside the bar:

IRISH WAKE
MEMORIAL
LAST FLIGHT WITH
STEVE WATSON
TUESDAY, FEB. 19, 2002 (3PM)
THREE ROSES BAR

I talked with Steve's longtime girlfriend. She told me how he died, on their apartment couch while taking a nap. He was a foreigner, so an autopsy was required and he was taken to the police hospital. Because Steve and the girl never married, a family member's permission was required for there to be a cremation. She told me that Steve had a brother, a sister and three children by two marriages, and none of them was coming to Thailand, although she'd talked with someone and whoever it was agreed to send the permission by mail.

She asked me if that's the way it was in America: a man died and the children turned their backs. I asked if Steve had been close to his family. She said he hadn't talked to anyone in years. I said many families were stubborn and unforgiving. I knew I was using words she probably didn't understand, although the English classes that Steve paid for had made her conversant and she was able to sound out printed words. In Thailand, I said, even when parents and children didn't talk, when someone died, the family came together. In America that wasn't always so.

She looked at the sign on the wall and asked, "What means 'flight'? Like 'helicopter'?" I said yes, like helicopter. Today was Steve's last helicopter ride.

By four o'clock, the bar was packed with expats, all of them getting drunk, toasting a photograph that had been placed on a small shrine over the bar, a mug of Carlsberg next to a small card that gave the dates of his birth and death. (He was fifty-five.) I looked around and thought that when I died, I'd be lucky to draw a third the number.

Hero/Entrepreneur

John Everingham? Isn't he the guy who swam across the Mekong River with his girlfriend tied to his waist to escape the communists in the seventies? Didn't Hollywood make a movie with Michael Landon and Priscilla Presley?

Well, yeah, and I'll get to that soon enough, but that was thirty years ago and when you ask John about it today, his genial smile might fade and he may wonder if he should politely change the subject to the breeding snakes. If you want to get his attention and hold it, ask him about when he helped blow the whistle on the CIA and its involvement in the Southeast Asian opium trade. Or ask him about that "high-tech, controlled-climate facility that regulates temperature and humidity, is escape-proofed, hygienic and monitored by cameras for security against theft" where he is breeding those rare Asian vipers and pythons that he keeps near his apartment and office in Bangkok. Or how he built a magazine publishing empire in Thailand that allows him to spend, on average, three of every four weeks traveling to some of the most exotic destinations in Asia, from Sri Lanka to Papua New Guinea.

Or, ask him how it all began, back when he was a high school senior in Brisbane, Australia, hating school and authority and itching to "see the rest of the world." His childhood wasn't unhappy. His father, a television engineer and amateur boat builder, introduced him to the Great Barrier Reef and his mom tolerated his keeping the longest snake in Australia in the yard. Still, his older sister "did all the right things, and I did not," he says, and in 1966, before he finished his senior year of high school, he dropped out and left home to work as a laborer in the sugar cane fields in Queensland.

"It was famous as being the toughest job in Australia," he says today, "but also the highest paying labor. I was sixteen and they thought I wouldn't last more than a few days. I finished the season, three months, with three layers of blisters on my hands."

Next, he went to New Guinea, where he claimed he was twenty-one and got a job as a bar manager. Eight months after that, with a plan to drive to Europe on a motorcycle, he went to Singapore on a cargo ship, bought his bike and drove it north through Malaysia, Thailand, Laos and Cambodia, leaving it, in early 1968, in Phnom Penh. He then took a plane to Saigon, arriving during the 1968 Tet offensive, a turning point in the Vietnam war, when it finally became clear to the world that the United States might not win.

While in Cambodia, he found some molds for temple carvings and hired someone to make charcoal rubbings on rice paper, paying him few dollars apiece. He then took them rolled up in a cardboard tube on a bus to Saigon, where he sold them for twenty to a hundred dollars each to "the wartime nouveau riche who wanted to take something authentic home." After that, motivated by little more than curiosity, he bought a camera on the Saigon black market and joined a group of freelance combat photographers.

As history would show, Vietnam was the last war where the press was given complete access to the front lines and the military thought it cool to cooperate. "All you had to do was show up at the airport and you could get a ride on a military flight," John says. "In three months, I went out forty nine times, selling my pictures to the news agencies in Saigon for fifteen dollars apiece. By the time I was twenty, I'd been in Vietnam for two years and my mind was radically changed. I no longer thought the war made any sense and I went back to Australia to see my parents, though I didn't now consider any place home."

That was in 1971. He'd been gone five years and now was of an age when he was supposed to register for the draft. He told friends he was ready to go to jail rather than go back to Vietnam to fight, so he didn't register and when he learned of a weekly flight to East Timor from Darwin, where no one checked identities on exiting, he joined the pack of war resisters fleeing Australia.

Entranced by the camera as a tool for telling stories and wanting to stir the anti-war pot, he went to Laos where after exploring hill tribe villages, he settled in Vientianne, the "deceptively peaceful" capital. "You could smell the war, but there were no bodies," he says. "The Lao people were so sweet and gentle. They didn't know what was going on, didn't understand capitalism or communism. I started doing some writing, and after a while I was hiring myself out by the day to work with visiting journalists because I could speak some Lao and sort of knew my way around."

This was when he met Alfred McCoy, who was researching *The Politics of Southeast Asia* (1972), a book now regarded as one of the best ever written about international drug trafficking. John told McCoy that he'd seen opium loaded into the CIA helicopters and took the writer into the hill tribe villages where the poppies were grown, getting caught in the crossfire in no man's land. As the communists approached villages, the U.S. told the residents to flee, and then, in John's words—in a report included in McCoy's book— the villages were bombed to "black stumps and scorched earth."

There came a time when John and McCoy and five others were ambushed and they ran for their lives. McCoy was overweight and collapsed climbing a hill, fell and told the others, "You go on without me, I'll die here." John pulled him to his feet and they all escaped unharmed. The next year, 1972, John's description of the village bombing appeared in *The Washington Monthly* as "Let Them Eat Bombs," another excerpt from McCoy's book, appeared in *Harper's Magazine* and, despite CIA attempts to suppress publication, when the book was released, it led the U.S. Congress to investigate the CIA's involvement in the opium trade. By then, John's friendship with McCoy was well known.

"I became very unpopular with the people who worked for Air America," he says. This was the secret U.S. air force that was the inspiration for a film starring Mel Gibson and Robert Downey Jr. "In a bar in Vientiane, a stranger came up to me and said, 'One day, we're going to kill you.' Not long after that, when I was in the field, a helicopter flew past me ten meters off the ground and an American inside made eye contact with me. The chopper then looped around to return and all I remembered was what the man in the bar said. I didn't know if it was coming back to offer me a ride or kill me. I was shit scared and ran as fast as I could, disappearing into a forest."

No attempt was ever made on his life by the U.S., but he was captured by the Pathet Lao, Communist Lao troops who mistook him for a downed American pilot. For four days he was held in a wooden cage, until a new officer on the scene asked to see the bag that was confiscated when John was taken prisoner. In it, he found cameras and a passport showing John was not an American, along with several articles he'd written about the horror of American bombs on poor Lao villages.

Believing that John was, in a sense, on their side, he was taken to the Plain of Jars and held for twenty-nine days. After the Pathet Lao took Vientianne, he became the only western journalist allowed to stay because of those articles. From 1975 to 1977, he provided stories and photos to the BBC and worked covertly for the *Far Eastern Economic Review, Newsweek* and NBC Radio. The Communists eventually realized what he was doing and that led to his arrest, a quick mock trial and deportation. In the process, he lost all his cameras and slides, but the hardest part was leaving his Lao girlfriend Keo behind. He would spend much of the next year trying to get her out.

His plan was to cross the kilometer-wide Mekong River that separated Laos from Thailand with SCUBA gear and return with Keo tied to his side, as she didn't know how to swim. Details of the escape were sent to her with someone who worked for the United Nations. When John crossed was critical, because in June the monsoon rains would begin, causing the river to deepen and widen, and the current to grow swift. He made his first attempt in April and swam away when he saw a crowd of picnickers on the sandbar where they'd planned to meet.

On his next try, in May, when he broke the surface, there was a boat full of men in uniforms nearby. By the time he tried again in June, half the sandbar was submerged and the current carried him past it. Now the river was so dark with silt, visibility was reduced to inches and John had to feel his way across on the bottom with his fingers. Finally, he surfaced and when she didn't see him, he called her name. She dashed to him and was lashed alongside.

"We were moving downstream toward a military outpost," John says. "She was terrified. I had a spare mask and an 'octopus' regulator for her, so she could breathe from my tank, but she panicked. I was wearing a belt with an extra loop, so I tied her to my side, face upwards. That way she could see daylight and that worked for her. I swam as hard as I could, finally crossing into Thai waters. I blew some air into an inflatable vest I was wearing, I was so exhausted I quit swimming, and we floated with the current, free and safe. Someone pulled us into a boat."

While the legal aspects of their escape were sorted, John was held in Thai jails, Keo in a refugee camp. That's when John received his first call from Hollywood. Friends in the media had sent his story around the world and a producer wanted to turn it into a movie. Michael Landon, star of TV's *Bonanza* and *Little House on the Prairie*, played John, an little-known Asian actress was cast as Keo, and Elvis Presley's widow, Priscilla, in her first big film role, portrayed John's American girlfriend. The film, released in 1982, was called *Comeback*, and when it was broadcast on TV, *Love is Forever*. John was disappointed and so was virtually everyone else.

This event would dog John for the rest of his life. But John wasn't looking back. He took the money he was given and opened a restaurant in Bangkok with a friend from Vientiane, an Indian named Cha Cha, who'd been a kitchen boy for Lord Mountbatten in the last days of the Raj and then a diplomatic cook for Indian ambassadors around the world, finally settling in Laos where he had his own restaurant.

Settling in Bangkok, John returned to writing and photography, stringing for an Australian newspaper and selling stories through his old friend at *National Geographic* and now was the magazine's editor. One of the articles was a collaboration with Denis Gray, the Associated Press bureau chief who broke the story about John's heroic swim. For four months, John photographed the subjects of the story, the King and Queen of Thailand. Later, when the magazine devoted an entire issue to Australia, John wrote a story about Matthew James Everingham, who had arrived on the first boat full of prisoners sent from England, in 1778. John said his ancestor worked for a London barrister and stole two law books when he was fired. When he finished his sentence in Australia, he was offered twelve acres of land or passage back to England. He stayed and John says there are now eight thousand Everingham descendants.

By 1985, John had a line of post cards across Thailand including Phuket and thought the island might support a magazine, so he started one. "I thought having my own magazine would give me more freedom," John says. "It was a delusion. After that, and as I started more magazines, I watched my freedoms slip away. I had to become a businessman instead of a photographer."

Following *Phuket* magazine came tourist guides to Phuket and Samui (the sort distributed free and supported by advertising); an inflight bi-monthly for Bangkok Airways, *Fah Thai*; a quarterly inflight for Siem Reap Airways, *Sarika*; and another quarterly, launched in 2003, *Asia-Pacific Tropical Homes.* He also published annual periodicals for Samui's travel board and for the Cambodian government and, in 2004, introduced Thailand's first magazine for water sports enthusiasts, *Siam Marine.*

John says it hasn't been easy and anyone who's worked with him, either on his staff or as a freelance contributor to one of his periodicals, will agree. All say he's a great guy, but payment frequently is low and slow, and sometimes it is supplemented in what is called "barter." That means you might get paid partially in cash, the rest in airline tickets, multi-star hotel rooms or meals in good restaurants, *that* coming from advertisers who give him coupons instead of baht. That said, John wants it known that when the Thai economy collapsed in 1997 and magazines all over Asia lost as much as half their advertising, and dozens of them closed their doors or declared bankruptcy, he did neither. As two-thirds of all publishing companies in Thailand went belly up, he says, he still advanced money to writers when he could.

He's proud of this, but there is nothing that seems to delight him more than his collection of snakes. By mid-2004, he had thirty of them near his flat overlooking the Chao Phrya River in Bangkok and in his home in Phuket. As is true with any snake handler, he is bitten often—the week before one of our recent meetings, his arm to the elbow was the size of his leg and purple—but that seems to him a small price to pay for the joy of breeding the third-largest serpent in the world, the Green Tree Python (found from Indonesia to New Guinea), the Burmese Golden Python, and The Wagler's Viper.

"The laws and the ways people think are strange," he says. "There are only eleven snakes in Thailand on the protected list and I'm forbidden to own them, even if I'm trying to increase their number. People talk about not killing stray dogs, yet they kill all wild animals, including the country's other 180 or so snake species. Serious collectors of snakes are trying to bring snakes into the mainstream, like dogs and cats."

John's marriage to Keo ended years ago—a son by the marriage, who uses the name Ananda Eve, is a star in Thai movies—and he is now married to a woman he met in 1995 in Kunming, China. Jade is the daughter of a doctor and an earthquake engineer, has a masters degree in marketing from Thammasat University, and is what John calls "one of the senior people running his company."

Though his time as a photographer has been cut to seven days a month, on average, his level of excitement seems little changed. Ten years ago, he had the first para-glider in Thailand, from which he gained the elevation that photographers usually can't get unless there happens to be a conveniently situated tree or building near what he wants to shoot, or he hires a prohibitively expensive helicopter.

"It's just an engine that I strap to my back, with a para-glider sail overhead," he says. "I can pack it in a box, throw it in the back of the car and once I'm in the air, travel up to thirty kilometers an hour. I can see the world the way a bird sees it. I can fly over the tops of trees and pick the leaves as I go by with my feet!

"I enjoy what I'm doing," he says. "I'm traveling three-quarters of the time, from Sri Lanka to Papua New Guinea [the territory covered in the homes magazine], I spend a lot of my life eating and drinking in very nice restaurants, staying in very nice hotels, mostly on barter accounts. Plus, I have the reward of seeing the magazines come out. I've worked my butt off, seven days a week, but I've created a nice lifestyle."

Rock Star

"Sometimes I feel like a motherless child/a long way from my home."

These song lyrics were translated into Thai by Rick Montembeault, the American singer/songwriter and rhythm guitarist for a Bangkok-based band called Flow. The words say a lot about his self-imposed exile in Thailand, but perhaps it is more telling that the song was a hit for Richie Havens in the United States back in the 1960s, an era Rick and his band members keenly feel a part of, although all were born long afterward.

In many ways, Rick and his band are an anachronism, some forty years out of step. The sound, lifestyle, and attitude match those of "garage bands" I was writing for *Rolling Stone* in Los Angeles when the magazine—then a tabloid newspaper—was young, in 1968. Flow is a band that recalls the exhuberant and insistent rhythms of the Summer of Love and its members—Rick and two others from the U.S., the fourth a Thai—with their long hair and the physiques of men on a brown rice diet, need only tie-dyed tee-shirts, bellbottom trousers, a string of beads and the scent of ganja and patchouli oil to make the picture complete.

The "hippie look" is not unique to Flow. Carabao and the Sounds for Life bands and Lam Morrison, popular in Thailand from the 1970s onwards, adopted the same hairy, jeans-and-head-scarf look, along with clear musical lines that lead back to what in the West in the Sixties was called "protest rock." And there are other expat bands in Thailand that play rock and the blues, but they are what Rick disparagingly calls "hobby bands" whose members all have "day jobs."

Flow, he says proudly, almost defiantly, is the only expat band in Thailand that survives solely on its music—never an easy feat anywhere, and in Thailand surely close to impossible. With no record company behind them—the band members record and market their own CDs—and a never-ending scramble to find venues that will pay them enough to put petrol in their van, it's a wonder they keep going at all. Some might call this self-imposed poverty. Rick calls it commitment.

Rick was born in New Hampshire, the descendant of French Canadians, in 1968—the year after the Summer of Love, the year when Bobby Kennedy and Martin Luther King were killed. As a teenager, he took guitar lessons for six months, quitting because he wanted to learn how to play the Beatles songs he heard on an older brother's record, and his instructor favored "Yankee Doodle" and "Turkey in the Straw." Eventually, he taught himself to play every instrument in his high school orchestra and was selected for the McDonald's All American Marching Band to perform at the Orange Bowl and later was named to go to Tanglewood for a summer, but his father, a self-employed machinist, didn't have the money to send him to either one.

So he shifted gears, deciding to study acting and was one of forty accepted out of fifteen hundred applicants to Boston University, dropping out in his sophomore year, again for lack of money, to take a job in a bookstore that had a music annex. "That's where I read your Jim Morrison biography," he told me. "I devoured everything from that era. This was in '88, '89, around there, and all the books coming out then were about

Woodstock, the Beat Generation—your generation—and it was the music I was listening to anyway, so I read everything I could about it. Bill Graham's biography. Everything about the Beatles.

"I listened to a lot of Crosby, Stills, Nash & Young, Buffalo Springfield, the Byrds, Jefferson Airplane, Santana. My contemporaries were playing punk music and I was trying to school myself in the roots. People didn't have purple hair in New Hampshire, didn't have safety pins in their ears. I grew up twenty years after the Beatles broke up. I missed all the hype, the Beatlemania thing. But I remember finding this Beatles record in my older brother's collection, being intrigued by the cover, putting it on and it made me feel good, it was uplifting. Punk didn't leave me uplifted at the end of the record. It was good for a cathartic release from anger, but I didn't need that. The cornerstone of my being is joy."

He even sounded like a flower child. Yet, if that was a fair characterization, he still lacked a garden into which he could sink his roots. He remained in Boston for four years, recording his first demo tapes with money from his dad, and then walked away from that city and after spending a winter in Vail, Colorado, went to Los Angeles in 1991.

"I'd done all I could in Boston, there was no music scene there. One of the things I believed about the Sixties was that there was a sense of community, camaraderie, there wasn't so much competition. All my friends in college went to LA, I thought what I was looking for might be in California, so I went there, too, and I found a group of people wrapped up in the coffee house thing, which was very strong in the Nineties."

For a while Rick played with a band called Ceramic Buddha, but again he was disappointed. "The record companies weren't interested in fringe music. Ask most people what their favorite color is and they pick a primary color, like red. And we were a magenta band." There also was a surfeit of groups; in LA, bands stood in line. "There were a lot of clubs, but every night there were seven bands playing at each one. You'd get ten, fifteen minutes plus five minutes to get your gear on and off the stage. It wasn't like Bangkok, where later I discovered that everybody used the same equipment. In L.A., every guitar player had to have his own computerized network of shit that he has to play through to get his sound that he thinks is different from the next guitar player who sounds exactly like him. The drummer wasn't going to let the next drummer play his snare. How are you going to develop in that sort of scene?"

That was when Peter Fleischhacker, a childhood friend from New Hampshire who was playing bass with Rick, got a call from his twin brother Roland from Thailand. Roland, who had lived in Southeast Asia for about four years, said he'd booked some gigs in Cambodia and Vietnam and asked if Peter and Rick would like to join him. With that phone call, for Rick the gates finally swung open on the mystique of other places, other cultures, on "otherness" itself...and in 1997, they found themselves in the artists' colony forming in a small club called the Beehive, near Bangkok's Chatuchak weekend market.

It was there that Rick met Gai Deepracha, whose very name, he points out, translates as "good people"—a man who as a teenager learned to speak English and play the guitar in a Bangkok jail and upon his release in 1969, migrated illegally to the United States. There, Rick says, continuing what already carries the tone of a stoned Sixties epic, he became a hippie, got deported back to Thailand, had a daughter with a woman who was half Thai and half Indian, divorced, then married a Swiss woman and went with her and his daughter to Switzerland. After divorcing again, he returned with his daughter to Bangkok. Rick met the daughter, Nampeung—Thai for Honey—and she and her dad became his first Thai friends. As Rick recalls the tale, you can almost hear the sitar cry.

It was also at Chatuchak that Rick met Supharit (Mit) Witchitwatee, a percussionist who'd played in several blues bands. Now the instrumentation was complete: lead guitar (Roland), bass (Peter), rhythm guitar and voice (Rick), and drums (Mit).

"The band's name came from our looking for signposts, flowing through life, how your life is a journey," Rick says, again sounding like a Sixties refugee. "Flow is like gravity and it will lead you exactly where you want to go. In L.A., trying my hardest to get noticed in the industry, trying to make a career, I couldn't get past the barriers. Once I came to Thailand, I found that just by letting go, I could get what I needed. There's something organic in that, something natural, the way things progress if you allow them to progress."

So, finally, as originally planned, the band went to Saigon, where they played at the bar named for the movie *Apocalypse Now*. When they shifted to Phnom Penh, they were caught up in a coup and their shows were cancelled. Returning to Bangkok, they learned more bad news: while they were stranded in Phnom Penh, the Asian economy went into the toilet and the musicians discovered what little money they had was almost worthless due to the currency devaluation.

"Something was trying to tell us we should stay," Rick says. "The truth is, we couldn't afford to leave!"

In 1999, something else happened that brought the Sixties attitude home again, when Mit was in a motorcycle accident on Koh Samui, where a physician suggested amputation of a leg. Rick and Peter took him in a van to Bangkok, where he spent twenty months in and out of a hospital and underwent eleven operations. It was almost two years before Mit returned to the band, after reinventing how he played the drums by holing up in a room every night with his practice kit. In the States in 2001, at the time of Mit's accident, most bands would have replaced their injured drummer. Rick and the twins didn't do that. They were a Sixties band, recalling when musicians were loyal musketeers, brothers with a sense of fealty they felt was missing four decades later, and Flow performed as a trio until Mit was able to kick the shit out of that bass drum again.

"We're the first ones to do what we're doing," Rick said. "Lots of the musicians in this country have a contract somewhere as an English teacher or something. You think they're fulltime musicians, but they're teaching aerobics at some hotel or something like that. The band is their hobby. We're the only fulltime original band, pushing its original stuff as its focus. There's never been an American rock band come to Thailand and write original rock and roll songs in Thai and record them. There aren't any true independents. We're the only ones doing grassroots recording. There are other so-called 'indies,' but they're either just small versions of the biggies or they're owned by the biggies."

Eight years after Chatuchak, the band called Flow was still flowing. By Western standards, they seemed stuck in the slow lane, but not by theirs. Flow was the only *farang* group that ever opened for Carabao, arguably the most enduring Thai rock band. They'd recorded and released two CDs of a planned trilogy—*Seeds* in 2001, *Roots* in 2003; *Flowers* was promised for another couple of years down the line—and were still working the small clubs as a headliner, all this while struggling with Thai rules that made it difficult for foreigners to work in almost any field, and especially in entertainment.

"We have to fly under the radar," Rick told me in 2003. "We're told we have to have work permits, but to get one you're supposed to have a specific address where you work, but we don't play at one place for, like, three months at a time and most foreign bands that work in Thailand—most of them 'copy bands' from the Philippines that can play note-for-note Beatles songs without an ounce of soul—that's what they do. We don't. We play original music and original songs, one night here, another night somewhere else."

A year later, Rick said the band was leaving Bangkok for Samui, where the almost out-of-control tourism development had created enough clubs to guarantee regular work. Rick and the twins also had been promised work permits by a Thai company organized to provide concerts nationwide, taking Flow under its corporate wing as employees. In Bangkok, Rick and his wife and their three-year-old son lived with her parents and on Samui, they'd be faced with rent and he'd have to buy a motorbike to get around.

He thought he could still survive. "The cost of living is so cheap I can afford to be a musician here. You can get paid shit and survive. I make a thousand baht every time I play. That's my income. The band may get ten thousand, twenty thousand for the gig, but each of us takes only a thousand. The rest goes into buying equipment, building our business. In Bangkok, some months I made only three thousand baht [$75]. It's hard to raise a family on that, but it's impossible to raise a family on that in the States. But, hey, the weather's good and you don't have to worry about a lot of things that you have to worry about somewhere else.

"In LA, while waiting for a gig, I worked as a waiter. Every weekend I'd be serving food and drinks to Jon Voigt or Robbie Robertson. I knew I was always going to be a waiter to them. When I got over here and people asked what I did and I said I was a musician, there was a look of respect in their eyes. Which you don't get in the States unless you're rich and a rock star. When I got over here, I was treated like a rock star. Without actually being one.

Rick thinks of himself as the band's "cheerleader," yet in the end, his cheerleading flags. "In some respects, we've gone as far as we can go. We need to attract people who can take us to the next level. Some of these people are not here, or just pass through. Also, when my son gets to a certain age, I want him to have a good education. I'd like my son to go to the same school I went to, same school my father and my grandparents went to, but still be a rock musician, sell lots of records, and know there's going to be a royalty check four times a year, and my family's going to have a roof over its head. I can't imagine doing what I'm doing now when I'm sixty." I interrupted, saying that I bet Mick Jagger said the same thing. "Yeah, that's probably true," Rick said, "but he doesn't still have to carry his amp."

He resumed his positive rap. "Every year, it gets a little better, we make a little more money, we're still growing. We still have tons of goals. The major goal is to keep going, to be able to survive doing what I love to do and not having to be a waiter to support it. I have very simple tastes. I don't need a big house in Bel Aire. Where I envision myself is being in the same league as the people I admire. How I get to that place, that level, I don't know."

This innocence—optimism without a plan—is redolent of the Sixties, too.

Class Clown

I was drinking beer at the bar of the Foreign Correspondents Club of Thailand with Jim Eckardt when four young Thai women took seats at a table nearby. Jim said he knew one of them and went to say hello. After a few minutes of talk, as part of what appeared to be a friendly departure, he grabbed his shirt-tails and raised them to reveal his enormous belly and rolled his stomach muscles from top to bottom and back again. It appeared as if an entire pig beneath that expanse of furry flesh were trying to kick its way free of its confinement.

I was as amazed by the gesture as I was startled by its crudeness. How, I wondered, would anyone know he could do that and, once knowing, why would he want to? When Jim rejoined me at the bar, I pretended I didn't see the feat and it wasn't until later, while reading one of his six published books, that he attributed this peculiar "talent" (his word) to his teenage years when he executed one-hundred sit-ups every night to reduce a small pot belly. "It didn't work," he wrote. "But I was left so riddled with inner muscle that I can undulate my entire stomach from sternum to abdomen." Like a belly dancer, he said, surely less than seriously.

Jim is a big man, just under six feet in height, with heavy limbs and that "huge, protruding, gelatinous, obscene excrescence of a gut" (again his words), the well-tended product of a self-described powerful and providential thirst. Picture Fred Flintstone, only slightly better dressed, and hairier.

Jim also lacks top lateral incisors, something else I learned from his book, "so my smile presents a pair of lethal fangs to the world. This is a family trait on my Bavarian side, which one dentist told me comes from the Huns," he went on. "I've explained to my wife about the Huns, who were a famous civilizing influence upon the Roman Empire…"

I had known Jim for nearly a decade and we were meeting at the Correspondents Club to celebrate his falling off the wagon, an annual event. Just as he gets his hair cut and beard trimmed once a year—he swears this is true—he also quits beer for 720 hours, a full month, every year, an act he said harked back to the eight years he spent in Catholic seminaries when such acts were called the "Mortification of the Flesh." The year previous, he told me, he went from 228 pounds to 206; this year, sadly, he started at 232 and fell only to 218. Still, he invited all his friends to come to the club to share a jar or two and, if your eyes were turned in the right direction at the right time, whenever he thought he had an audience, to witness his remarkable Belly Roll.

"When you have a body like mine," he said, "you have to have a sense of humor."

And a sense of humor this longtime American expat certainly has. In two novels, three collections of autobiographical rambles, and a collection of personality profiles, as he barreled through what he calls a "checkered and rather improbable life," he seems to have been amused by every thing, every place and everyone, not least of all himself. And to hear him tell it, the forty or so years of misadventure have been fueled across five continents almost entirely by drink.

However, for those who think James Eckardt, one of the early baby boomers—born in 1946 in New York City, his father German, his mom Irish, his grandparents on both sides immigrants—is no more than an amiable hack, a drinker of staggering capacity with a guitar that he calls a "Crowd Dispersal Weapon," will have misjudged him. To give too much credence to the tales of his seemingly endless "weekend wallows" with friends he calls "louts and tosspots" and far worse, is to miss much of the man.

For instance, Jim said he really did think he wanted to become a priest, entering a Carmelite seminary in the aptly named Middletown, New York, at thirteen. Three years later, he was expelled for a "bad attitude." Translation: class clown. Two more seminaries followed, the last two years wearing a cassock and Roman collar while studying epistemology, phenomenology, ontology, metaphysics, ethics and theology, and learning to read in Latin and Greek. He graduated with a BA in philosophy. He then "bailed," leaving the path to priesthood forever, along with half of his class.

The vow of celibacy was part of it. But, he said, "I wanted to get out. The seminary got me out of the suburban world and now I wanted to be an expatriate. I'd read Hemingway and Fitzgerald and I wanted to see the world. Fuckin-A, I did!"

But so long as he remained a seminarian, his summers were devoted to public service, setting a course that would carry him through much of his adult life. In 1965 and 1966 in Alabama, he was what segregationists called an "outside agitator," registering voters in Birmingham at the time when a Negro church was infamously bombed by the Ku Klux Klan, playing guitar at Mass in a section called Dynamite Hill, where Angela Davis and Condaleeza Rice grew up. A year later, in 1967, during the Summer of Love, he worked with a Puerto Rican street gang in Brooklyn.

After graduating, he signed on as a yeoman on an old liberty ship, crossing the Atlantic twice, worked in a hospital emergency room in one of Brooklyn's meanest neighborhoods, drove to San Francisco and back with the guys and girls of his Alabama crew. He then joined the Peace Corps in order to escape the draft and Vietnam and was sent to Sierra Leone, a West African country he later said "looked best through the bottom of a beer glass," where "you were sort of parachuted into the bush from whence, two years later, you emerged thirty pounds lighter, with a malarial complexion, myriad bush sores, and fascinating intestinal guests." There, he lived thirty miles from the nearest electricity and helped build roads, raised chickens and rabbits, and had his "second childhood," bodysurfing whitewater rapids, jumping off a three hundred-foot-high waterfall, and started across Africa on a motorcycle, a trip that was aborted halfway when his mom was diagnosed with cancer. He went home and got a job in Manhattan as a Peace Corps recruiter, soon sending himself to the Amazon for another eighteen months of wilderness and deprivation.

While in Africa, he and a fellow Peace Corps volunteer had daydreamed about sailing around the world, so when that friend asked Jim to come to the Philippines to crew for him in a trip back to the west coast of Africa, he kissed his Brazilian sweetie goodbye and went. In Jakarta, after surviving a near capsizing in the South China Sea, Jim jumped ship and started writing *Alabama Days* in Singapore, a novel that would take five years and six drafts to finish, and which, after he sold it to a major U.S. publisher, remains unpublished to this day.

After living for six months in Malacca, he bought a motorcycle and drove to Thailand for a cheaper life, settling in Songkhla, near the Malaysian border, where he met and married Mem, the daughter of a local cop. After a honeymoon on his motorcycle back down to Singapore, Jim took his bride to Mobile, Alabama, for a year, where he continued working on his novel and Mem got pregnant. When his wife returned to Songkhla to have the baby, Jim then embarked on a five-thousand-mile motorcycle journey to visit a friend in Newfound-land, rejoining his wife in Thailand in time for the birth of his first daughter, Elizabeth, in 1977.

For the next fifteen years, Jim remained in the small beachside town, living in twelve houses ("lotta times because of a fight with landlords; Mem has a mouth on her"), adding a fluency in Thai (southern dialect) to his Puerto Rican Spanish, Krio (the lingua franca spoken in Sierra Leone), Timne (an African tribal tongue), Brazilian Portuguese and Malay, and falling in with a mixed bunch of locals and expats who played beach volleyball and spear-fished and drank themselves goofy on the weekends. During the week, Jim taught English at a nearby university for eighteen months, then worked for the American Consulate for twelve years, interviewing and writing State Department cables about Vietnamese refugees, an experience he drew upon for another novel. He also fathered two more daughters, Linda and Erika (1978 and 1987), and started freelancing stories about his family and friends to the *Bangkok Post*.

In the first, he told about the time his wife threatened to remove the most "sensitive" part of his anatomy with a knife—"a misunderstanding," he says—and in another he wrote about her dragging him before the cameras of a Thai television show, telling outrageous lies about him in an attempt to win a big cash prize. There were accounts of his Songkhla volleyball team's crushing the Hash House Harriers ("the drinking club with a running prob-lem") and of his third child, called "Erika the Beast," always best-ing him. He also worried, in print, what he might do if his fast-developing pre-pubescent daughter Elizabeth met a horny young man like he once was and got almost saccharine when remem-bering Christmases in the tropics. But seldom was a laugh far away, as when he took advantage of his dubious journalism cre-dentials to freeload in the best hotels (where he blended in "like Mike Tyson in the College of Cardinals"), and, another time, an old high school sweetheart came to Songkhla and met Mem, who at first was insanely jealous, but from the moment the old friend from New York told Mem that Jim had been "just as big an idiot as a teenager as he is today," they bonded like sisters.

Eventually, Jim would write some 180 reminiscences, collecting many of them in his first two published books, both taking the names from stories inside, *Waylaid by the Bimbos* and *On the Bus with Yobs, Frogs, Sods and the Lovely Lena.* He also wrote two more novels, *Boat People* and *Running With the Sharks*, both of which would be published locally but not for several years.

When the consulate closed in 1992, Jim moved to Bangkok to take a job with a monthly "business and lifestyle" magazine called *Manager*, leaving his wife and a family that now included a fourth child, a son, Patrick (1989), in Songkhla where his oldest was in a government school with a scholarship. Over the next five years, he was a "Big City journalist," writing 174 stories—many of them profiles later collected into still another non-fiction book, *Bangkok People*. Those people were part of what led him to conclude that Bangkok was one of the great cities of the world.

"Bangkok reminds me of what Dr. Johnson said about London: a man who's tired of London is tired of life." Jim also was making more than $2,500 a month at *Manager*, a small fortune in Thailand, and was still selling stories to the *Post* and teaching a private course in cross-cultural management. For the first time in his life, he was making more money than he could spend on the customary basics and beer.

Not that it changed his lifestyle. He continued to live in a ten-foot-by-ten-foot room in the Peachy Guesthouse ("the classiest flophouse in Banglampoo") for seventy dollars a month, a room furnished with a bed, a desk and a chair ("the same décor of the Catholic seminary where I was an inmate twenty five years ago"), even sharing it for a year with his oldest daughter while she went to school in Bangkok. While around him, predictably, he gathered another noisy group of boisterous drinkers. The "second adolescence" that he said began in Africa and continued in Songkhla now entered its third decade. "Just because you're middle-aged," he told me, "doesn't mean you can't be immature."

Jim said he became a writer because he read so voluminously from high school onward, starting and abandoning a novel when he was still in seminary. "Like any writer," he said, "I think my life is extremely important and I should write about it. It's ambition and a need for money, of course, but more than that, it's a stab at immortality. I wanted people to read about me and my friends, like Hemingway in *The Sun Also Rises*. There is a joy in writing, the best of it coming when the characters start talking to each other and all you're doing is taking dictation. Thai shadow puppet masters say they're not making up the stories they tell, the puppets are doing the talking."

Of course, he exaggerates in telling his tales—many raconteurs call this "embellishing"—and he does it mainly for comic effect, almost always making himself the butt of the joke. Thus, his rambunctious tales may be at conflict with the facts, but never inhibited by them. He says, "My motto is, 'What is the fragile flower of truth before the onrushing steamroller of a good story?'"

It's said that alcohol destroys brain cells, but Jim's memory is as improbable as his life. Six or eight beers into an evening, he remains eloquent, or at the very least coherent, about existentialism, can still recite St. Thomas Aquinas in Latin, and tells you why Robert Stone's *A Flag to Sunrise* was like Joseph Conrad's *Nostramo*, but better, and then marches out the characters, plots and dialog from other novels by the score.

In time, of course, Jim's fortunes turned again, when the Thai economy collapsed in 1997, and as a consequence, *Manager* was shut down and the *Post* stopped accepting freelance material. For a time, Jim worked for the *Phuket Gazette* and *The Phnom Penh Post*—described in *The Year of Living Stupidly: Boom, Bust and Cambodia*—and then he went through a period of desperate, freelance joblessness. (Prompting him to tell friends a tired old joke: "What's the difference between a freelance writer and a street corner hooker? The hooker gets paid on time. And she gets more respect.") His family, meanwhile, had moved in with Mem's father in Prachinburi, two hours north of Bangkok.

In 2000, the tide turned again and Jim was hired as a sub-editor by *The Nation*, one of Bangkok's two English-language daily newspapers. That meant he edited the editorial and opinion pages while reviewing books and writing travel stories. This allowed him to buy a small house in Prachinburi, fix it up and lease it to an uncle, and then move his family into a big rented home with an "American kitchen, marble and parquet floors, and a view of mango orchards and rice fields that go to the horizon." He then started commuting on weekends.

His oldest daughter, Elizabeth, was studying to be a nurse in 2004 in New York, intending to stay. Linda, who survived a brain seizure at age eight, was twenty-three and a Buddhist nun in her third year of university. Erika, who turned into a "perfect child" when she reached school age and thus stopped qualifying as fodder for his stories, and his son, Patrick, were both teenagers and still in school in Prachinburi.

Once more Jim had the best of two worlds: a rural lifestyle on the weekends, weekdays in a city he adored, working for the daily newspaper that was most vocally anti-government. (Jim compared *The Nation* to a pirate ship attacking a Spanish galleon laden with gold and crooked politicians.) And…so as not to give anyone the impression that he'd gone upmarket, in Bangkok he lived in a single room across the highway from his office where there were ducks and chickens and wood houses, paying thirty five dollars a month.

Lonely Planeteer

Joe Cummings was a young guitarist in the United States whose band, the Fog, opened shows for Blue Oyster Cult, Edgar Winter's White Trash, Uriah Heep, and other bands of the 1970s, but then his bassist and drummer killed themselves and following a severe attack of mononucleosis, Joe lost all power in his strumming hand. That's when he joined the Peace Corps and was sent to Thailand.

Thailand wasn't what Joe Cummings expected. The man who later would write the country's *Lonely Planet* guide for more than twenty years, and thus arguably became the expat most readily identified with the country (at least by non-residents), arrived in the Land of Smiles in 1977, believing it would be, in his words, "peaceful, chilled out, no tension, a social paradise with Buddhism underpinning it all, everyone getting along and being super polite."

The truth he encountered was the opposite. Only months before, when students demonstrated against the return to Thailand of a former military dictator, police and right-wing paramilitary civilian groups attacked a group of two thousand students holding a sit-in, killing and injuring more than a hundred. It was a time of virulent anti-communism and at the university where the Peace Corps assigned him to teach English, books were burned merely because they had "red" covers.

After one year, he dropped out of the Peace Corps—as a volunteer, there were no contracts and he says the classes were boring—and following visits to India and Nepal and spending another short spell in Thailand, he returned to the United States to get a masters degree in Thai language and Asian art history at the University of California at Berkeley, returning again to translate two books by a noted Buddhist monk as part of his thesis. That was in 1981 and he's spent at least six months of every year in Thailand since. In 1996, he gave up his official U.S. residency and six years later was determined to become a Thai citizen, as he continued to write new books and every two years update guides to Thailand, Chiang Mai, Bangkok, Thailand's Beaches and Islands, and Laos.

"What kept me coming back was the extreme tolerance...flexibility is a better word...of Thais and Thai society," he says. "I love the way they can accommodate extremes. I like the idea of saving face. What drives a lot of *farangs* bonkers I love. *Farangs* think the politeness is fake, that it's better to be straight and honest and express yourself. I'm not that way. I'm non-confrontational, too. My only inclination was to be like the Thais."

Buddhism exerts another pull. For several years he owned a house in Mexico and contributed to the *Moon Handbook* guide to that country, but he missed being able to walk into a wat to meditate or find a monk to whom he could talk. Today he calls himself "reluctantly dependent on Buddhism," because it goes against his "free spirit" past, when he regarded organized religions as anathema—but he also calls himself "as Buddhist as ninety nine percent of Thais."

Joe is what's called "rangy," the sort of guy Hollywood would cast in a western movie, so tall and lean you wonder if he's eating regularly, or is on one of those brown rice diets popular in the 1960s. As many who came of age in America's hippie era, his lank, brown hair hangs to near shoulder length, he dresses as casually as most of the backpackers for whom the *Lonely Planet* guides originally were written, and his proudest possession is the 1957 Fender Telecaster guitar that he plays when he jams with Thai and other expat musicians, mainly in small Bangkok and Chiang Mai clubs, where he sometimes calls himself "Slimfinger Turnpike." (A visit to a Chinese acupuncturist in Bangkok in 1977 returned the strength to his hand.)

Perhaps the high of his many highs in rock came to him not through playing, but in taking Mick Jagger on a tour of the Chao Phrya River in 2003, when the Rolling Stones were to play a concert there. On his Web site (http://www.joecummings.com), he recalls being nervous, but "Mick was, to sum up my overall impression, eternally hip and surprisingly introspective. We talked one-on-one for two hours…and he was charming, witty and easy. He gave me some brotherly advice on life, fame and love."

(Several years ago, Joe also joined a Javanese *gamelan* band at the University of California at Los Angeles, learning in eighteen months to play virtually every instrument, from gongs to xylophones.)

Although seventeen years separate our ages, our shared interest in music, food, Thailand and writing created an easy bond when we met. We didn't become fast friends, but more than acquaintances. When he was writing the superb *World Food Thailand*, another LP publication, he interviewed me on the subject of Thai street food because I'd co-written a book about it. When I said I thought visitors who didn't eat food on the street because they were afraid of getting sick—when, in fact, that was where the best and most varied Thai food was—should stay home, he thanked me and said he wished he could've said that. As a guidebook guru, telling people to stay home was not cool.

So, yes, he said when I asked, some of the freedom he had to write what he thought when the Thailand guide and the Lonely Planet organization were smaller is now gone. As the Thailand guidebook has grown from 128 pages to 986, and the company has become the most successful travel guide publisher on a no-longer-so-lonely planet, freedom of speech has gone the way of unspoiled beaches in southern Thailand. Lonely Planet is a big liability target now, and Joe says if he tries to warn readers about rip-off travel agencies, his bosses worry about lawsuits. They also told him that the page and a half that he devoted to prostitution in the book's tenth edition, published in 2003, was excessive, said it made LP look like it was advertising the sex venues that operate so openly.

There was as much or more prostitution in many other places, including the United States, Joe says, but in Thailand there is "more visibility and society tolerates it a bit more, so there's not so much of a stigma attached to being a prostitute or going to one. Thais don't think it's such a big deal. There are two sides, of course. Lonely Planet says I'm writing too much about it, but many of the readers call me Mr. Prude or Reverend Joe and ask why I don't write more about the bar scene. I wrote several editions of the guide to Burma and people asked whether it was politically correct to write about travel in Burma the same way they asked if it was politically correct to write about prostitution. It's a tightrope, it's very difficult to walk the line."

More criticism came when he was accused of contributing to environmental damage to islands in the south by calling attention to the unspoiled resorts. At first he said he was surprised, because "it was such a spurious argument that's so easily countered. If a place is beginning to happen, it's gonna get out, somebody is gonna talk about it. The responsible thing to do is write about the place sensibly, to talk about the social and environmental impact we all have, but you can't save a place by not writing about it. That's number one.

"The second thing is people don't really follow my advice. The restaurants I recommend, the ones I say this is where you get the real stuff, I go there and I'm the only customer. They go where everybody else hangs out, wherever is close to their guest-house and has an English menu. For years, I said please boycott Koh Phi Phi because they're destroying the environment, and year after year I'd go there and there were tons of *Lonely Planets*. I've been recommending the Northeast forever, telling people this is one of the best ways to experience real Thai culture, and it's cheap, which ought to attract the backpackers. It has great architecture, it has all these national parks, the food is good, and yet, statistics show only two percent of all visitors go there."

So Joe just "does his thing." Every two years, he spends three months researching and another three months writing updates for his books, sometimes working on two or more at the same time, while farming out the tedious check-every-guesthouse grunt work to what he calls "interns," because it's now an unrewarding grind.

"There are between four and five hundred places to stay on Koh Samui," he said. "It's total tedium and it's no longer Thailand. It's sort of Thai, you can make an argument either way, but as far as what I get out of it, I don't feel like I'm really in Thailand."

About half of each year he's traveling and he said he never tires of that, and if he now spends some of his nights in five-star hotels, he also doesn't mind sleeping on bedding that looks as if it hasn't been washed lately. Joe is on the high side of fifty now, an age when you begin to take stock and check out the prostate, while you still try to figure ways to find a publisher to let you write another book about Asian art and architecture (as he did about Burma's) and find another nightclub that'll give you a platform for bluesy finger-picking.

It's too early to retire and so long as he stays on the road, it's the travel that'll pay the bills. His guide to Thailand is one of most popular in the Lonely Planet pack, selling between seventy thousand and a hundred thousand copies a year, and is either Number One, Two, or Three annually in LP's "rolling twelve" bestsellers—the others being China and India—with more than one and a half million copies published since the first edition in 1981. His best-selling book, *Thailand: A Travel Survival Guide*, sold more than a million copies and has been translated into half a dozen languages. Joe gets a royalty on all his works except the Chiang Mai book.

Ironically, it is in the northern Thai city where he lives, sharing a three-bedroom, three-bath condo with a new Thai wife whom he describes as an "incredible cook." Most of the people he spends his time with are now Thai, he said, and he eats *farang* food only two or three times a month.

"Once I tapped into Thai cuisine, I couldn't get along in the States. Everything outside of Thailand seems too bland or too heavy. Thai cuisine suits me. It's got penetrating taste and yet it fits in the body nicely." He further said in his book about Thai cuisine that its "light and healthy nature, vast internal range, adaptability to other cooking styles and straightforward stovetop dynamics, raises it well beyond the ken of just another 'ethnic cuisine' to be struck off a list of palatal destinations. Today Thai cuisine has become so globally appreciated that in a survey polling travel agencies in over twenty five countries, it ranked fourth after France, Italy and Hong Kong in perceived excellence of cuisine."

Joe said he lives in Chiang Mai because "it's closer to Thai society's roots" and because he can drive across town in twenty minutes, as opposed to the hour or more it takes to travel the same distance in Bangkok. Bangkok's name "explodes off the tongue and pumps a dank steam into the mind," he said. "The city draws together the essence of everything that is sacred and profane in Thailand. The city continues to suck in rural Thais, international investors, and curious visitors from around the world with its capacity to fuse the carnal, the spiritual and the entrepreneurial. Bangkok's legendary tolerance lends equal support to the monk and the playboy, to the beggar and the Benz dealer."

Chiang Mai's expat community may not be as interesting as Bangkok's, he went on, but it tended to be more fluent in Thai. It was also cheaper to live in Chiang Mai. For a couple of years, he said, he'd been making a comparative study and figured just about everything cost half the price in Bangkok.

Born in 1952 in New Orleans to a military father and a mother also serving in the U.S. armed forces, the wandering bug bit him early. For ten years, he says, he lived on or near bases in Europe, while the image that is most vivid from his youth is of traveling with his sister and his parents, his dad at the wheel, his mom reading a book about the next destination.

Teaching Eng-Lit

One of the things that many Thais have in common with native English speakers is that they all have trouble speaking the language properly. The difference, according to John Quincannon, a fulltime teacher of English in Bangkok, is that the Thais seem to be trying harder. At least those with money are. Even if they don't really want to.

John didn't leave his comfortable job teaching in a university in the United States to become a teacher in Thailand. He left because he was bored witless. He says he enjoyed Thailand the two times he visited during university holidays, so in 1987 he sold everything he owned and got on a plane with one suitcase, no friends in Thailand, and no job.

"I wanted something different," he says, "and Thailand seemed to offer that."

For five years he drifted, ticking off Thai provinces on a map as he visited them. He was living on $700 a month from his savings and as the bank balance fell, he was thinking about going home when in 1992 he met someone in a bar in Patpong who said his office was hiring. The office was that of the Orderly Departure

Program (ODP), a little-known operation funded by the United States to interview, evaluate and, if considered appropriate, relocate Vietnamese refugees to the U.S. following the end of the war. Many of them were "Boat People," asylum seekers fleeing Vietnam in crowded, rickety vessels who frequently fell prey to pirates or drowned at sea.

"If we interviewed anyone considering that means of departure, we told them don't take the risk, stay in Vietnam while we process your application," John said, "and if you qualify, we'll pay your way and set you up in the U.S." It was an offer few could refuse.

Today John recalls there were a dozen or more refugee categories acceptable. Vietnamese who had worked with the Americans during the war and subsequently spent years in prisons and "re-education" camps. Amerasians, the children abandoned by U.S. military men and now were scorned by their fathers' former enemies. Catholic nuns, Buddhist monks, journalists, poets, former South Vietnamese military officers, anti-Communist war heroes, and children and spouses and parents of Vietnamese who'd fled during the last days of the war. People the newly re-united Vietnam were glad to be rid of.

Sometimes, John says, ODP processed as many as ten thousand in a two-week period. By the time the program was shut down in 1998, he and his co-workers had helped move more than half a million, mainly to Texas and California—among them, one of Larry Hillblom's "wives" and a child she had with the DHL chief. The waitress from Nha Trang and her son didn't qualify for the ODP program but it was a case that the U.S. government told his office to expedite, fearing that once the youngster was given the millions of dollars awarded him by a court following Hillblom's death, the Vietnamese government might levy some extraordinary taxes.

John loved it. His office was in Saigon, renamed Ho Chi Minh City when the war ended in 1975. It was a city of decaying but still romantic old French colonial buildings, the streets filled with bicycles and motorbikes, with foreigners pouring in after 1989 when the government announced a welcoming policy called *doi moi*. An American named David Jacobson was running the Q Bar, and nearby a hole-in-the-wall named for the movie *Apocalypse Now* anchored a block-long strip of joints where young Vietnamese women entertained the big, pale foreigners as, perhaps, their mothers had a generation earlier. It had the feel of a boom town, yet kept its provincial charm. John traveled to and from Bangkok, earning a comfortable base salary plus seventy dollars per diem when in Vietnam.

"My unit manager was an Annapolis graduate, a Vietnam vet who served on the USS *Kitty Hawk*," John recalls. "Others had Peace Corps ties. Some people, like me, were just bored with where they were from. Others wanted to do something different between getting their bachelor's and master's degrees."

After six years, the dream job ended, when the U.S. opened an embassy in Hanoi that assumed responsibility for all further relocations. For four more years John was adrift in Thailand, living off a dwindling savings account. He was fifty-six years old and it was time to re-evaluate.

His parents had been government workers, too—his dad an FBI fingerprint technician, his mom one of J. Edgar Hoover's secretaries. ("No," John volunteers, "she never saw him wearing a dress.") His father served in the U.S. Army in Europe during World War II and after the war, settled with his wife in Lake Geneva, Wisconsin, where John was born, in 1946, the second of four children, "Baby Boomers" born at the rate of about one a year. With his brother, just eleven months younger, he had a rambunctious relationship; one time when they fought it was with a hammer and a baseball bat, and both were later taken to the emergency ward. Because his mom was one of seventeen children, he had more than a hundred first cousins; many he never met.

When John was six, the Quincannons moved to North Carolina so his mom could be close to her family and it was here that John was educated. His dad stayed in the Army reserves, worked for the Western Electric Company, and went to night school to get a master's degree. When John was drafted, in 1969, he said he was content to go in as an enlisted man. His father encouraged him to go to Officers Candidate School. What followed in Vietnam, he says, was another snooze. He remained behind the front lines, where "it was mostly drudgery and boredom, waiting for the unexpected." The most exciting it got for him, he says, was when some Playboy bunnies came with the USO to entertain.

After returning to the States in 1972, he went to Europe for six months without an itinerary, visiting Germany, Spain, Morocco and Scandinavia. That done, and still not knowing what to do with himself, John returned to North Carolina State, earned a Master's degree in economics, taught that subject while working on his doctorate until he got bored again. That's when he decided to pull the plug on his job, his PhD, and his career, all for a taste of fantasy. That's when he went to Thailand, drifted, worked for ODP, then went into automatic drive again, and when another four years passed and he was as desperate for work as he was determined not to go "home" again, he took a two-week course that got him a certificate as a teacher of English.

By now, English had become—as one jokester put it—"the *lingua franca* of business" worldwide. In Hong Kong, India, Malaysia, Singapore and the Philippines, which earlier were colonies of English-speaking powers, English already was a "second language" for a range of practical functions in government, law and education. Not so in Thailand, but in the boom of the 1980s that made Thailand's economy the fastest growing in the world, parents started sending their children to English-speaking countries for their education and demanded more English instruction at home.

At the time, teaching English was regarded by many as the native English speaker's last stand, something foreigners did when they reached the point where they'd do anything just so they could stay. In a country where teachers generally were revered, in contrast the teaching of English to Thais was, and continues to be today, remarkable for its low salaries and its dubious esteem, a refuge for native English speakers who find many jobs are off limits to foreigners.

At the same time, many Thais think they *should* learn English, or have parents who make that decision for them. It isn't always the way they'd like to spend their after-school hours, evenings, and weekends, though, and often what results is a sort of shotgun wedding between East and West, where both the teacher and the taught would rather be doing something else.

"There's a lot of pressure on the kids to score high in entrance exams so they can get into Chulalongkorn or Thammasat Universities," John says. "A high school student will study English every day in school, then study two more hours of English language computer or get one-on-one English tutoring in the afternoon. It's unbelievable. I feel sorry for them. I have students six-, seven-, eight-years old, they study three hours after school and on weekends they have instruction in ballet and tennis. I had a class yesterday with five children under the age of six. One was sleeping, two were fighting, another was hiding under his desk. And their parents say I don't push them hard enough, tell me I should be assigning more homework and longer essays."

These are the children of wealthy, ethnic Chinese, who dominate Thailand's business community and control much of the military and government. An identical story has unfolded in Kuala Lumpur, Singapore, Jakarta and Hong Kong, where in just two generations—their ambition driven by clannish cooperation, thrift and tireless energy—they have clambered, like ants, to the top of the heap.

"Their grandparents were born in China, their parents in Thailand, they live at home with both parents and grandparents, and sleep with their parents until they're eight, ten, maybe twelve," John says. "They go to the best schools. They have never taken public transportation, they have drivers who take them to school and pick them up, and if they don't have drivers, their parents do it, sometimes right up through university. They have never had a friend whose father was a policeman or a bus driver. The only poor Thais they've met are their maids. They come to my classes with their nannies, who sit with them and bring food to make sure the kids get something to eat during breaks. The nannies wipe their mouths and carry their book bags.

"The girls are little princesses. They don't know how to cook, can't even boil water for noodles. Many have no siblings. They never play outside, it's too hot. Instead, they go to air-conditioned malls, to shop and show off their new wardrobes. Even the six-year-olds know not to go outside, because the sun might darken their skin. I asked one girl if she'd ever been to Isan [the poor northeastern part of the country] and she said it was uncivilized, why would anyone want to go there? She was sixteen."

John says the company that hired him, The International Inlingua School of Languages, is at the "top end" of the crowded field, a thirty-year-old company with headquarters in Berne, Switzerland, and 250 branches worldwide. There are fifteen classroom locations in Bangkok, where John usually works seven days a week, often for twelve hours a day, instructing school students during the week (many of them one-on-one but others in classes of up to fifty) and Thai employees of multi-national companies like Daimler-Chrysler, DHL, Pfizer and Caltex Oil on the weekends.

For this, he is paid by the hour—and thus gets no work permit and no benefits—earning, on average, 55,000 baht [$1,375] a month. This is a grand sum for a Thai and while it is enough to pay for the small apartment he shares with his Thai girlfriend of six years and cover his beer bill at the Hog's Breath Saloon near-by, it leaves little for anything else. When he leaves the country every thirty days to get a new visa, he does so as quickly as possible to keep his lost work days to a minimum.

Yet, he insists he enjoys his job. He likes the challenge of teaching people—whose native language is without tenses or articles or capital letters, who drop the "s" or change it to a "t" sound at the end of words, lose the "r" sound nearly everywhere, and change the "l" to "n"—not only a new language, but also how to change the way they speak.

"Even those whose grammar is good," he says, "their pronunciation is usually pretty bad, even if they've studied in the U.S. They emphasize the last syllable of words, so that, for instance, the Oriental Hotel is pronounced 'Orien-TEN Ho-TEN' and the Central Department Store chain is 'Cen-TEN.' 'Tennis' becomes 'ten-NIT.' An 'a' is added to some words, as well, so that 'steak' is pronounced 'sa-TEAK.' And your name is 'Jerr-EE Hop-KIN.'"

This is called "Tinglish" or "Thaiglish." In the age of globalization, polyglot is not unusual. There is not one English language, there are many English languages, from the "Singlish" that mixes Chinese with Malay and English in Singapore to the creole patois common from Hawaii to the Caribbean.

John loves this and says a return to North Carolina—where "goodbye" is pronounced "y'all come back, y'hear?"—no longer is an option.

The Collector

How many men who are now fifty years old or older got their first exposure to "sex" in the pages of *National Geographic* magazine? Thousands? Millions?

Now, answer me this: how many of those men went beyond the photographs of bare-breasted natives and read the stories as well and became explorers and adventurers?

Jason Schoonover may be one of the few. He, like the generation that followed that bought *Playboy* for the articles (or so they said), admits he enjoyed the illustrations—the only other "soft porn" available to him at the time was in the lingerie section of the Canadian Sears catalog—but he swears that he *read* every issue of the *National Geographic* ever published, leading, eventually, to a career tramping some of the most remote parts of the world and membership as a Fellow in the world-renowned Explorers Club.

A native of Saskatchewan, born in 1946, Jason (originally Harvey; he changed his name later because he hated Harvey), was the son of a man who delivered milk and ran the local livery stable. "The farm, et cetera, failed when I was four and my father moved onward and upward to becoming a horrendous drunk, rising all the way to skid row in his later years, a total failure at everything." He and his sister, he says, thus effectively were raised by their mother, a second grade school teacher.

They lived in Carrot River, a frontier town (pop. nine hundred), in a house heated by a wood-burning stove, water fetched in buckets from the well, "where wheat fields meet a virgin birch, pine, and poplar forest that runs north eight hundred miles to the Barren Land's tree line. It was in that boreal forest beginning two blocks from our home that I fell in love with Nature and the outdoors and where I feel most at home."

Following four years of English Literature and History at Simon Fraser University outside Vancouver, he became a popular radio personality and started freelancing for newspapers, magazines, and the Canadian Broadcasting Corporation as well as the stage, writing, directing, and producing retired Prime Minister Diefenbaker's eightieth birthday gala at Saskatoon' Centennial Auditorium. He also owned and operated Saskatoon's first taped music DJ operation, investing his profits in income-producing real estate, founding Schoonover Properties in 1975. Since 1977, he boasts, he's been "gainfully unemployed." His travels to more than fifty countries are paid for by the revenue from his rental property. From a high of eight multi-unit properties, he now has a single family dwelling and four duplexes, most of them in Saskatoon's prime university area, all managed by a professional company that does that sort of thing.

In 1978, on his first solo trip around the world, he says, "I found myself staying in a dollar-a-day room just inside the jungle in a village in Sri Lanka. Like out of a movie—no kidding—drums were beating in the distance in the jungle night. I asked the owner what they were. 'Devil dance, sar,' he replied. 'Devil dance? Is it possible to see it?' 'Of course, sar. I'll be happy to take you.'"

For the next two months, Jason assembled a collection of ninety seven masks, costumes, drums, whistles, bells and other ritual paraphernalia, along with sound recordings and photos. He sold the fully documented collection to the University of British Columbia's Museum of Anthropology and when the Smithsonian Institution asked him to assemble a similar collection, he jumped at the chance to make this his new career, moving to Bangkok.

From 1978 to 1985, Jason sold a dozen collections to a half-dozen museums around the world, from Germany to Japan, some under contract, other times on speculation, also selling to individual collectors and antiquity and primitive art shops across the U.S. and Canada. His contacts now secure in Sri Lanka, most of these items were devil dance artifacts, although one collection focused on Tantric Buddhist and folk trappings from Nepal, Tibet and Assam, and another that included masks from Indonesia.

"On average, my major collections sold for $12,000, with the largest to a Japanese museum for $17,000. The markup was generally eight-and-a-half times the field price, but there were exceptions. I remember an Indonesian mask I paid five dollars for that I sold as part of a collection for $175—so the profits were good."

Still, he concluded that the market was thin. "There were 350 ethnological museums in the world but only two handfuls had any money, and many of them were already stocked with Asian ethnography or the curators had other interests. Once I had filled the existing holes, those markets dried up." It was time for another career change.

So he invented an alter ego named Lee Rivers and wrote a novel called *The Bangkok Collection*, published in Canada in 1988, republished world-wide a year later by Bantam in New York as *Thai Gold*. "Rivers's specialties are eastern antiquities, exotic women, and high-priced danger," the American edition crowed on its back cover. The bearded author's photo showed him in a snakeskin jacket and the paperback mentioned memberships in the Explorers Club of New York and the Foreign Correspondents Club of Thailand. He was single, the blurb continued, and "lives comfortably out of a burgundy Samsonite and a khaki knapsack and can most often be found somewhere in Asia."

Indiana Jones, step back! There's a new guy in town, and this one—Lee Rivers—was, by Jason's admission, taller and more courageous than himself, but not quite as smart. Maybe that explains why in the book and in a sequel, *Opium Dream*, published in Thailand in 2002, Rivers has a running dialog with his penis, an appendage he calls "Ol' Thunder." A third novel, *The Manila Galleon* was to be published in 2005.

Despite, or maybe because of, outrageous characters and plots, the novels were pretty good. One reviewer called *Opium Dream*, a story that takes Rivers to Afghanistan and the long-lost burial site of Kublai Khan, "a fast-paced Robert Ludlum-meets-Steven Spielberg romp," an opinion not far off the mark. Once the reader made the leap of faith required by many novels (and films) in this genre, *Dream*, like it's predecessor, was an action-packed fun ride from Saigon to Cairo that, unlike many others in the field, made few mistakes; most fiction set in this region was so riddled with glaring errors it was clear that the authors spent only a little time there or were hurrying to meet a deadline. By 2005, Jason had been a visitor or part-time resident in Asia for more than twenty-five years and was proud that the descriptions of culture and place, from the Golden Triangle to Afghanistan, invariably rang true.

Jason continued to divide his time between Thailand and Toon-town, as he called it, where he shared his home in the same upper-middle-class, university neighborhood with Su Hattori, an Intensive Care Unit supervisor he often called the Imperial Dragon Lady.

"Old, quality-character homes and doctors, lawyers, professors and businessmen, and even a few artists, predominate on either side of the boulevard," he said. "We're one block from the river and in the position where local gal Joni Mitchell stood to paint the painting on the cover of her second album. We have 2,575 square feet, which is a bit small, but only because of all the anthro junk."

Much about a man's character is revealed by such stuff when it's used to feather his nest. By his own description, Jason's home is more like a pack rat's than a bird's.

"Guests are usually agape at our house because it's like living in an anthropological museum," he says. "Where tribal art doesn't cover the walls and floors, there's original prairie art and a series of Kama Sutra renditions done on wafers of elephant ivory. One room features over eighty authentic masks. We have Neolithic stone tools from Laos and Burma; a bronze age axe head from Vietnam; textiles from several hill tribes; framed tropical insects; a collection of about a dozen 2,500-year-old Mother Goddess terra-cottas from Sri Lanka; basket work from several Southeast Asian tribes, including three over four feet tall; king cobra and alligator skins; shields and spears framing the fireplace. Sherpa walking sticks; Buddhist statues; a dozen-piece collection of Vietnamese water puppets; and dinosaur bones. And nothing is new or "touristo," although he insists nothing is really valuable and the security system in his home is to discourage kids from trashing his place while swiping his stereo.

"Collecting is in my bones. I've never thrown anything away, from my Boy Scout hat to the baseball glove I got in Grade Four to the beads on the Cree moccasins I wore in Grade Six. Elvis's and the Beatles' first album covers are pinned to the ceiling of the guest room where a net on the wall displays more than 125 antique fishing lures. I'm a collector of damned near everything. But my museum collecting days are over. Ethnography just doesn't command the prices that archeological artifacts do and I don't move in that market, for which I have ethical misgivings.

"Unlike centuries-old stone carvings, ethnographic items are rarely over a hundred years old, most often just a few years or decades, and invariably still in production. For example, a new mask can easily be carved to replace the one I acquired for a museum where the hardware and software—the documentation—

of the cult will be safe and saved for posterity. If the twentieth century was a steamroller on these subcultures, this one will flatten them completely within the next couple of decades, highlighting the urgency that they find refuge in museums or the fact of their existence will be lost forever."

Jason's story sounds like one he might have read in his beloved *National Geographic*. When he talks of other valued possessions in his home, he begins to sound like an article in *Outside* or *Guns & Ammo*. "Our flatwater and whitewater experiences in our seventeen-foot, six-inch Kevlar Hellman canoe with ash trim and two-wood, laminated, twenty-six-ounce paddles wholly tune me up for another year," he says. "But I also love drinking beer and fishing and own an old tub with a steering wheel and a thirty-five-year-old, thirty-three-horse Johnson. Stomping around stubble fields and golden-leafed forests soaking up the rich autumn aromas while stalking game birds with my .12-gauge Remington 1000 semi-automatic shotgun is another enormous pleasure. I also have a beautiful-fitting and smooth lever-action Savage .243 for big game; a backup Winchester 2200 .12-gauge pump which is a piece of shit; an Enfield .30-.06 (the caliber used on Martin Luther King) for big game like elk and moose; a Mossberg .16-gauge, model 190 shotgun for grouse which is more of a collector's item, the gauge not having adequate punching power; and, finally, a .22 Cooey semi-automatic for popping the heads off grouse. I shoot for the table, not the wall. There's nothing as delicious—and healthy—as sizzling Bambi steaks…"

He's also a gastronomical adventurer. Once when the geese he was hunting didn't come, "I got bored and when a crow flew over, I blasted it. Crow tastes and has the texture of a tire—and I even slow-roasted it—like a steel-belted Michelin summer 205/60 R-15 sports car tire." Of a record grasshopper year on the prairies, he said, "Many people thought I was nuts sweeping them into my specimen net. Straight into the boiling water, and they turn red like lobsters and have such a delicate, delicious flavor!"

In Thailand, his life is somewhat more confined, austere, but the image of a man thumping his chest like one of Diane Fossey's gorillas remains. In Bangkok, he stays in small guest house rooms, where he boils his drinking water on a hotplate, eats many of his meals on the street, wears rumpled safari suits and cheap Hawaiian shirts (always in sandals and shorts), but he also roams afield, returning to Sri Lanka for more devil dancing, crewing on a friend's yacht in a race in the Andaman Sea. He calls himself a "half-time expat" and makes it clear that as much as "I absolutely love Canada's fabulous summers and autumns," which he spends in the outdoors, that at the first sign of snow and cold–both "four letter words"–he runs "shrieking in terror to the airport and a plane back to that beautiful sauna that is Asia."

"Thailand is simply the most beautiful, exotic country on the planet, and the only one that's truly and wholly livable. If it weren't for Thailand, life on this planet, with its too, too restrictive cultures, would be unbearable. Although Canada is sheer heaven in summer, it's seven shades of hell in the winter. Islam is disturbing; Hinduism is an eye-roller; and Christianity has been a two thousand-year scourge on Western civilization. The prissy, politically correct part of our Western culture disgusts me.

"Thailand, on the other hand, with its tranquil, laissez-faire Buddhism and lazy pace has its mind wide open, the way the rest of the world should be in so, so many ways. Thailand has perfect–hot!–weather and beaches and beautiful jungle and fascinating hill tribes and, hell, the whole culture is focused on pleasure, such as with its incredible cuisine and massages. I never really knew what the word 'exotic' meant until I came to Thailand. Plus, it attracts the most fascinating, adventurous people in the world–outside of New York City–and they all end up washing back drinks at the Foreign Correspondents Club. Other people who live their dreams live here. I can relate to that."

Renaissance
Pleasure Hog

His calves are the size of small watermelons, his buttocks prize-winning pumpkins and his belly protrudes like a barrel of hard cider or beer. He sports a black bandito mustache, his hair is pulled back into a pony-tail that falls to the middle of his broad back. There are tattoos on many parts of this large anatomy, and it is no shock that he enjoys motorcycles and owns a beer bar in Bangkok.

What may be surprising is that Dennis Cooper fancies himself an aging flower child; when you ask for his business card, he may give you one that beneath his name it says "Advice, Forgiveness, Pearls of Wisdom, Secular Humanist," a throwback to his days as a sort of clownish monk who got paid for "Advice, Forgiveness…" and etc.

Born in Rochester, New York, in 1958 and raised a Catholic, one of three boys and two girls, at seventeen he was vice president of the New York State Secondary School Students Association and expected to become a lawyer or a priest. As so often happens when parents entertain such misplaced hopes, Dennis took an alternate route.

When his fifteen-year-old girlfriend got pregnant and he needed money to help her, he concluded he had no marketable skills, so he joined the U.S. Army and was sent to Germany where he displayed the soldiering skills of Beetle Bailey. Assigned as a driver for officers, he regularly drove into trees and poles, prompting the officers to yell, "I'll drive!" He also learned that if he flunked three tests for drug use, the Army would give him a medical discharge. So he found a sergeant who used heroin and borrowed his urine for three check-ups, timing his discharge so that he wouldn't lose the educational benefits offered by the G.I. Bill. Soon he was back in New York and attending classes in a junior college. Then in 1978, when he was twenty, he accompanied a friend to something called the Renaissance Pleasure Faire and went completely off the rails. For life.

The Pleasure Faire in upstate Oswego, New York, was an annual event built around arts and crafts, dressed in a medieval theme with maidens on horseback, men in chain mail made out of beer can pull tabs who staged make-believe fights with wood broadaxes and swords, children dancing around maypoles, and stall operators dressed in tights and hats with feathers, shouting, "Forsooth! Saveth your money, spendeth here!" The first was held in Los Angeles in the late 1960s and soon they popped up like magic mushrooms all over the United States.

Dennis and his pal had learned glass-blowing when they were in high school, making marijuana pipes for their friends, so they took a booth, his friend blowing glass vases (and on the sly, an occasional pipe), while Dennis did the pitching. They had so much fun and made so much money, he says, "I haven't had an honest job since."

Traveling from Faire to Faire in the years that followed, he sometimes dressed up like Friar Tuck and called himself Brother Pompadour Twat, selling advice and indulgences for as much as a dollar. ("I gave pretty good advice, too," he boasts.) Ordained through the mail by the Universal Life Church, he also performed about a dozen weddings at the Faires, asking for a gratuity of a bottle of Scotch. Mostly, he and a partner operated the games: axe and knife throwing, archery, giant swings and carousels, anything that more or less fit the sixteenth-century theme.

"I'd work the shows myself, every weekend from February to November," he says. "I bought my first pair of green ladies panty hose with great embarrassment in Oswego and I've spent a total of three years of my life or more in costume since. After a while, we had three shows every weekend and we did everything from managing the games to stringing beads to mowing the grass and picking up the trash. We slept in our cars and friends' houses, but we made so much money I'd take a length of PVC pipe, fill it with cash and bury it under my house. I didn't want to run it through a bank."

How much cash? "I'll talk about drugs and sex," he says, "but I will not talk about money."

His home was then in Spencerville, Oklahoma, where a friend's grandmother grew marijuana in her yard, where, he says, "the pavement ends and the West begins." Dennis liked the feel of the area (near the Texas border) and he built the house where he and his partners would unwind at the end of the festival season, when it got too cold to romp around in tights. Soon, Dennis bought the Red Star Drive-In, a bar and restaurant that dated back to the 1930s. For three years, it was a place where customers brought their pet pigs (and sometimes rattlesnakes) and his fellow motorcycle club members rode in on Harley Davidsons. Dennis said they weren't supposed to open until noon, but as a courtesy to regular customers he opened at eight, and a local dentist actually set up shop and pulled teeth on the pool table.

This was when he got his first tattoos. "I first resisted, thinking it was a vain display," he says, "but one day I realized that vanity meant that the flesh was somehow sacred, which I didn't believe, and I decided to make my skin into a comic book. In the toilet, I routinely read the *Bible* quotations on my legs."

Weekends he continued commuting to the Faires, going to Kansas City and Dallas, and to Florida and New York, driving straight through in school buses that constantly broke down. "We'd spend four days at a gas station in Nebraska trying to get it fixed," he recalls. "Now we have sixty employees running the games and rides and we take three days to get from one location to the next, in trucks and trailers with walkie-talkies. It's not as much fun now.

"But we're still doing the same crazy stuff. Throw beanbags at coconuts. Try to climb a rope ladder. Yeah, I know, there weren't any coconuts in Europe, but when there's a lake, we run paddle boats and they didn't have paddle boats in the sixteenth century, either. But if we use enough burlap on the boats, it *looks* Renaissance."

Dennis said he also attended seventeen Mardi Gras weeks in New Orleans during the 1970s and 1980s, doing face-painting on riverboats and peddling alligator puppets on a stick and electric yo-yos and "head hoppers," those floppy antenna things you wear on your head, purchased wholesale for pennies, retailing for $4 apiece, all sold on the street from a borrowed supermarket shopping cart.

Dennis first visited Thailand in 1991, part of a six-month holiday that also took him to several other Southeast Asian countries, as well as to New Zealand and Taiwan. He kept coming back, spending most of his time in the Kingdom from 1997, and in 1999 he met a woman named Kamruen. A year later, after Dennis said he spent thousands of dollars every month on the phone calling her from the U.S. , they married. It was his first marriage, at forty-two. Before that, he said, he was a "serial monogamist."

Dennis and I met, briefly and mundanely, in a department store in upcountry Thailand when his wife and my then girlfriend (now wife), Lamyai, spotted each other. They had worked together in Bangkok. It was another year before Dennis and I got to know each other, meeting again at a Fourth of July picnic, hosted every year in Bangkok by the local chapter of the American Chamber of Commerce, a gathering where longtime expats who don't see each other during the year, reconnect and get caught up. Hot dogs and burgers, corn on the cob, apple pie and Budweiser beer; a patriotic speech by the U.S. ambassador; egg tosses, sack races, and a tug-of-war for the kids; fireworks; John Philip Sousa marches performed by the Royal Thai Army Band. That was when I learned about Dennis's connection to the Pleasure Faire. I told him I'd met an earlier wife at the Faire in Los Angeles.

A couple of years later, I ran into Dennis and Kamruen in my Bangkok neighborhood, one of several known for its hotels and bars and shops catering to foreign visitors. He told us that he was then spending only four months a year in the States, leaving the management of his Pleasure Faire empire in the hands of his capable partner, who preferred it that way. Since marrying Kamruen, he said, they'd shared an apartment in Bangkok (in a building where Lamyai once had a room) and he'd built a home for his mother-in-law upcountry in Surin not that far from our own, and purchased some land nearby for a house he intended to build for himself and Kamruen. He said he'd also just bought an interest in a bar, the Hang Out Pub, where I met him the following night.

Unlike the joint in Oklahoma, this one was so small there wasn't room for a pool table, forget about riding in on a Harley or pulling teeth. Dennis was seated at the end of the bar, his back to a large window that opened onto a narrow lane lined with condominiums and serviced apartment buildings, the source of his customer base. I slid onto a barstool next to him and we ordered mugs of Chang draft, one of the cheapest and strongest Thai beers.

"A simple beer for a simple man," Dennis said about himself.

Yes, he said, he still enjoyed the Pleasure Faire and had added a Renaissance Torture Chamber. "People piss their pants," he said.

"Kamruen [who accompanies him on his trips to the U.S.] will open a window and say, 'Boo!' and mom will pass out and the kids start crying. If you get somebody who pukes, you've done good!

"But the huge insurance costs drive you nuts. You're giving people a chance to hurt themselves. We've never had anyone badly injured, but I don't like the administrative part of it. Most people come for fun, but some come looking for a way to file a lawsuit. It puts you right off.

"The bar business is no better. Customers who got in trouble after leaving the bar come in the next day and blame me. And between moments of excitement—the fights—it's the most boring place in the world to be. Consider the people you have to talk to."

He has only a year or so to go on the bar lease, he said, when a hotel will go up on the land beneath it and the adjacent businesses, and soon after that he hopes to be living in Thailand fulltime, after selling his half of the Faire partnership.

"I don't feel judged here," he says. "In Kamruen's village, they accept me the same way I was accepted back when I started working the Faires and shared a house with seven other people and slept in my car. In America today, I feel like I'm being judged because of my appearance."

The only big problem he faced, he says, was what to do with the stuff he'd collected over the years. "Catholics are into statuary and iconography," he said, "so I collected Masonic stuff. I have forty fezzes. I have a complete set of *Playboy* and piles and piles of *Zap* comics. I have collections of poker chips, marbles, Indian artifacts (including an amazingly well preserved skull), trading cards, Christian iconography, cowboy stuff, good books and such pornography as I deem suitably weird. I gave all my 'freak' material to a friend who has a museum, but I still have a full container of stuff. I was going to bring it to Thailand, but what would I do with it? I'm ready to get rid of it all."

Dennis insists that he is a simple man. He may look like Man Mountain Dean, but he speaks softly and as we talked he said he was reading *100 Years of Solitude* for the fourth time; and he hasn't forgotten his flower child roots. When I told him about two friends, a cop in Los Angeles and a priest working in the Bangkok slums, saying they both dealt with the same kind of people, but viewed them from opposing points of view, he said, "Right, the cop expects the bad in the person and the priest looks for the good." There was no question about which of the two he identified with.

I told Dennis I wanted to include him in a book about expats who had interesting histories. "I am not one of them," he said. "If you're gonna get a story out of me, you'll have to pull and twist, and then make it up, because it's not there."

Real Life Forrest Gump

A lawyer visiting Bangkok from San Francisco, where he'd made a career representing the Grateful Dead and their nonconformist friends, after meeting Jerry Hopkins told him, "You know, you look like the straightest person I've ever met, but after what you told me about yourself, I'm convinced you're one of the most bent." Jerry liked that, and pointing to his close-cropped hair and gray beard, his button-down shirt, pressed jeans, and polished shoes, he merely smiled and said, "Camouflage."

Jerry thought it began in 1944, when he was nine and started reading the war dispatches from the Pacific bylined Ernie Pyle, a famous war correspondent. When he grew up, he decided that he, too, would travel the world, meet interesting people, and write about them. He hasn't wavered since and quoting both Thoreau and Frost, he followed a "different drummer" and moved along a "road less traveled." (Now you know where those clichés originated.) In this pursuit, he became something of what one day would be called a "nerd," for years reading only science fiction and fantasy and collecting such things as stamps and coins and seashells and birds' nests and rocks.

There was a Colonial quaintness about his hometown in southern New Jersey, where he lived on Friends Avenue and for the first seven years, attended Friends School, worshipped at the Quaker Meeting House at the end of the block and played during the winter in the hilly Friends Cemetery across the street, scraping the runners of his sled over the tombstones of his ancestors, who settled the village in the early 1700s. A slogan posted on all his Quaker school classrooms urged students to "Go the Second Mile"; if you were assigned one book report, it would be nice if you wrote two. Thus, Jerry said, he became someone who liked to "work." His parents ran a small dry cleaning business from their home. During the Second World War, his father was a welder in a shipyard, exempted from the draft because of a rheumatic heart.

Years later, Jerry told people that no one in his family, except in time of war, had traveled farther than fifty miles away. Once he saw what lay beyond, on a school holiday car trip to Florida with his brother and mother, he said there was no turning back. For him, the highlight of that journey came when they stopped at a circus tent with a sign that said "TWO-HEADED COW." It was a calf, dead and stuffed, but it did appear to have two heads, and was part of an old-fashioned "freak" show that now would be politically incorrect. For some reason, his mother gave him an additional twenty five cents to see the special attraction, a live hermaphrodite.

University in Virginia followed, where students pledged not to cheat on exams and honored a tradition called Conventional Dress. Jerry wore the required tie, but it was either bright orange or its design appeared as if someone had just vomited on it. He also became a Big Man On Campus, editing both the humor magazine and the campus newspaper, becoming known for his dark sense of humor and dissenting, liberal point of view.

After graduation, he worked as a reporter in North Carolina for a short time, was an ROTC officer in the Army, and then went to Columbia University to get a MS in journalism, taking a weekend job at NBC TV as a copy boy, while writing features for the then very young *Village Voice*. Graduating in 1959, he spent the next two years in New Orleans covering school integration, freedom rides and jazz. Then it was back to New York, where he lucked into a job writing and producing shows for Mike Wallace. It might be said that this was when he became Jerry Gump.

By now he was married to the secretary of one of his former Columbia professors, but it didn't last and when Mike's show was cancelled after a year, and the production company hired Steve Allen to star in a replacement series on the West Coast, Jerry was offered a job as the comedian's "vice president in charge of left-fielders," or "kook-booker." That meant he was responsible for finding someone who walked a road even less traveled than his own was becoming, one for each of the five shows recorded weekly: circus performers, health faddists, people who'd gone for rides on UFOs, nudists and the like. Many became good friends.

In New York, he'd met Paul Krassner, who edited a magazine of satire and when Paul visited Los Angeles, he staged "An Evening With..." himself, inviting all his subscribers, including numerous prominent comedians, most of whom Jerry had met during the course of his working for Steve. At the end of the evening, in one of those bizarre, Gumpish occurrences, he found himself introducing two of them, saying "Lenny, this is Groucho...Groucho, this is Lenny."

Steve asked Jerry to write and produce a television special that would introduce jazz to a young audience. Jerry decided he had to show the roots shared by jazz and rock—the blues—and began listening to rock radio for the first time. Soon after that, in 1964, the Beatles made their first tour of America and when Steve's show collapsed, Jerry started booking acts on a syndicated rock show and, for more than a year, dated one of the dancers, a wannabe actress who called herself "Terry Garr, Movie Star." At the time, all she had going for her was a Dial soap commercial.

And that's the way it went. Quitting television in 1966—because he didn't like the pressure, he said, although he enjoyed the money—he and a friend opened one of the country's first three "psychedelic" stores, or "head shops," the first in Los Angeles, near UCLA. When *Newsweek* wrote a story about the new phenomenon, Jerry said that on the basis of the first several months' revenue, they'd probably gross $50,000 that year. All over America, he told friends later, he could hear hippies say, "Hey, maaaaaan, let's open a head shop!"

Newsweek said he sold posters of rock stars and that drew a letter from a hardware store owner in Hibbing, Minnesota, who wondered if Jerry might have any of his son. The man's name was Abe Zimmerman and his son, Robert, recorded under the name Bob Dylan. It was a weird time, when he hosted the city's first "Love-Ins" and sold rolling papers to a UCLA basketball player named Lew Alcindor (later known as Abdul Jabar) and bought San Francisco dance posters from an out-of-work actor named Harrison Ford.

In less than three years, most of the product sold in head shops had been co-opted by mainstream stores and Jerry became the L.A. correspondent for a new tabloid called *Rolling Stone*, one of the "underground newspapers" he'd sold in his store. In the years that followed, he interviewed Jim Morrison and Frank Zappa and hundreds more, wrote a history of rock and roll, grew his hair to his shoulders, wore tie-dyed clothing and beads, smoked a lot of what was called "dope," got slammed around by the cops protesting the Vietnam war, lived in one of L.A.'s canyons across the street from a band called Captain Fuck and His Electric Baloney Sandwich (the Captain had worked in his head shop), wrote the text for a book about music festivals for two photographer friends, and at the suggestion of Morrison, wrote the first biography of Elvis Presley and, when Morrison died, accepted an assignment to write one about him.

By now, the writer was married again, to the daughter of a Beverly Hills real estate tycoon and a former Goldwyn Girl, with whom he had a daughter (in 1970) and bought a small farm in northern California to do what was then called the "back-to-the-land trip." This was interrupted in 1972 by another year with *Rolling Stone*, in Europe and Africa this time, when he toured the continent with the Grateful Dead, covered a gypsy pilgrimage in the south of France, wrote about motorcycle races on the Isle of Man, spent a week in exile with Tim Leary in Switzerland (on the lam from a prison in California), and wrote stories datelined Cape Town and Nairobi. He and his wife had a second child whose placenta he made into a paté, then served to his guests when they came to meet his son. Don't ask him why. He says he doesn't know, recalling the marvelous Grace Slick line, "If you remember the Sixties, you weren't there."

Back in California, he was arrested after sending a letter to Leary, who'd also been arrested and returned to prison. Jerry was accused of dosing the letter with LSD. The cops were looking for an acid factory on his rural road and they figured he and his wife were running it. Their lawyer argued that if a man sent a cake with a file to someone in prison, that didn't mean he had a file factory at home, a joke Jerry didn't think funny at the time. The lawyer then argued that because the cops had requested state confirmation of a field lab test conducted on the letter, and led the raid before the state tests came back negative, the illegal substances found during the raid were obtained by illegal search and seizure. The judge said that if Jerry and his wife had written anyone other than Leary...well, if he was wrong, a higher court would correct him and he found them guilty of possession of marijuana and paraphernalia (misdemeanors) and cultivation of some plants found in a window box (a felony). The superior court threw the case out and when Leary was released from prison and told the story, he said he thought it was hilarious.

In 1974, Jerry discovered his son was deaf and the back-to-the-land trip was over. He and his family moved to the San Francisco Bay Area, where for the next two years they lived in a seaside town and the boy attended classes for the hearing impaired, while Jerry kept the Jim Morrison biography in circulation (it was rejected by the commissioning publisher) and wrote an illustrated history of the condom. No one seemed interested in either one and in 1975, still living off the royalties from the Elvis book, he began researching an authorized biography of Raquel Welch. That was when his wife, returning from a solo vacation in Hawaii, said she'd met a guitar player and she wanted a divorce, but also wanted the entire family to move to the islands. They separated, Jerry went to Rio de Janeiro for Carnival with Raquel, and by summer 1976 Jerry and his wife were living in separate but more or less equal houses on the opposite sides of Oahu, with the kids shifting back forth fortnightly, as Jerry stopped listening to rock and roll and dedicated his ears to Hawaiian music. When Cameron Crowe, the teen whiz who started writing for *Rolling Stone* about the time that Jerry stopped and who later went on to write and direct movies (*Jerry McGuire, Almost Famous,* etc.) came to Honolulu and they met, he was high on the fact that he'd just met Bob Dylan. "Oh, yeah," Jerry said back, truly believing that his most recent coup was equal, "I've just interviewed the Makaha Sons of Ni'ihau!"

After the Morrison book was rejected by more than thirty publishers, Jerry decided to hang it up, telling Danny Sugerman, who was a Doors fan in the 1960s when he was about sixteen. By now there were two manuscripts, one the size of the Manhattan phone book, the other the size of the book for maybe Queens. Danny said he wanted to try to find a publisher and sent the long version to Warner Books, where previously it was rejected twice. This time, it landed on the desk of a young woman who loved the Doors and somehow convinced the editorial board to publish it. When Jerry met her some time later, he asked what she'd done before she was an editor. She told him, "Ten-thousand mikes of acid and two years in a commune in New Mexico." "Ah," said Jerry, "now I understand."

The publisher allocated no money for promotion, so Jerry and Danny booked the Whisky a Go-Go, the Sunset Strip club where the Doors were discovered, for a night and put their names on the marquee. They got the club for the night free, so long as they paid the bar bill. Both were broke, but invited about five hundred people. Tim Leary was sitting on Jerry's right, Lenny Bruce's ghost on his left, and the surviving Doors were on stage when a telegram arrived. Jerry took it to the stage and read, "Dear Jerry and Danny, Next week *No One Here Gets Out Alive* goes onto the *New York Times* list at No. 16. We'll pay the bar bill." It subsequently went to No.1, the first rock biography to do so, launching a new publishing milieu, remaining on the *Times* list for nine months, going back to No. 2 when Oliver Stone made a movie about the Doors in 1991, providing royalties that put Jerry's kids through college.

By now, there was a third wife, with whom he was sharing a fancy house in Honolulu's Beverly Hills. This was "crazy time," he told friends later, and "we were demonstrating all the worst signs of the newly rich, everything I once said I hated. Grass and Red Mountain were replaced by cocaine and Chardonnay. She adorned me with gold chains and a one-carat diamond pinkie ring. The kids went to the top schools. We had five charge accounts at the best department store, including gold and crystal accounts. Between us, we had ten credit cards. We spent weekends in five-star hotels. I bought her a BMW for her birthday. Mr. and Mrs. Hot Shit, headed for a fall."

They moved to Los Angeles for a year (1984) when Jerry thought he wanted to be a screenwriter, then fled back to Hawaii after hearing the joke, "Hollywood is a place where not only you must succeed, but your friends must fail." Jerry signed contracts for books about David Bowie and Yoko Ono, but the game was up. The cash was running out and he took what his daughter called a "real job," which meant he put on shoes and trousers and left the house in the morning instead of wrapping a sarong around his waist and going to the next room. First, he worked for a weekly business newspaper and then as a speechwriter for Honolulu's mayor during a re-election campaign. The mayor won and fired him.

During the campaign, Jerry was hit in a crosswalk by a driver who ran a red light, breaking his back, skull and left foot. While in the hospital under the influence of something that probably was illegal on the street, he decided that as soon as he could walk, he would and he told his wife that he was leaving her. They'd been to bankruptcy court and the separation surprised no one except the children. By now, Jerry's son had gone back to his natural mother, forced by Jerry's taking his wife's side against him. Jerry says it was the biggest mistake of his life.

For the five years following the divorce, Jerry lived in a two-room cottage a minute's walk to Diamond Head Beach, working for about half that time in economic development (trying to diversify the faltering Hawaii economy), the other half returning to freelance writing and sharing his bed with a Polynesian transsexual street prostitute, with whom he fell in love. He also made peace with his son.

In early 1993, following repeat visits to Bali, Thailand and Vietnam, and his first to Cambodia, and with another long trip planned for later the same year, Jerry realized that he would, by year's end, spend six months in Southeast Asia. He decided to move. He'd lived in Hawaii for seventeen years and was bored; he believed Hawaii was the most beautiful place on earth, but every day was the same, there were no surprises. His kids were grown and gone, he was single and the relationship with the transsexual was winding down. He had money enough to last two years, he thought, so he sold everything he owned at a two-weekend yard sale and in September, got on a plane with three suit-cases. At the time, he was negotiating with the Vietnamese gov-ernment to do a series of books about Vietnam, and contemplat-ed living there, but the talks didn't seem to be going anywhere (they didn't), and while spending several weeks in a friend's holi-day home in Bali, he decided to live in Bangkok.

Long before, he decided that he would spend the rest of his life between the Tropics of Capricorn and Cancer, so Thailand's cli-mate was right; the cuisine was his favorite of the many he'd tried; there was a relatively free press (something that couldn't be said for virtually any other country in the region); the politics, religion and lifestyle were strange enough to keep him baffled and entertained; the cost of living was low; and the women were as beautiful as the bars they worked in were uninhibited. He told friends that during an early visit to Vietnam, it was while he was sitting in a restaurant beside a river outside Saigon, eating catfish, that he realized how much he had in common with his lunch: they both were bottom-feeders. And Bangkok was a bottom-feed-er's paradise. He also believed that in Thailand he could be sur-prised again.

In the years that followed, occupying a one-bedroom flat on a leafy residential street, he worked on becoming a travel and food writer. He went hot air ballooning over much of Thailand, wrote about Komodo dragons and gamelan music in Indonesia, and twice traveled from Hanoi to Saigon, by hired car and train. He picked up monthly columns in a Bangkok magazine and the in-flight magazine for Thai Airways and for a year edited part of a web page for a Japanese advertising agency. For *Time*, he wrote a profile of Manila and for three publications reported on "blood tourism," the growing popularity of such events as the annual Easter crucifixion of Christians in the Philippines. For a regional daily based in Bangkok, he profiled regional personalities and went to Vladivostok for the same newspaper to write an article about what it's like to do business there in the winter, when the Sea of Japan was frozen to the horizon. His first trip to Burma produced five more stories and when the King of Thailand celebrated his fiftieth year on the throne, he sold several articles about the monarch's talent as a musician and composer. With photographers, he collaborated on a history of the Hmong hilltribe and a book called *Extreme Cuisine: The Weird and Wonderful Food That People Eat.* He also wrote a biography of an American Catholic priest who founded an orphanage and schools for the deaf, blind and disabled...and spent time most weeks with another priest in the Bangkok slums, with whom he was working on other books.

His fifth year in Thailand, he was hospitalized with angina pain and two years later had a triple bypass. By then, he'd met Lamyai, the daughter of rice farmers. Soon after his surgery, they built a house on her family farm, and in 2003 they were married in Buddhist and Christian ceremonies, in their country home and in a chapel in the slums of Bangkok. He was sixty-seven, she was forty-two.

Woody Allen said most of what determined what one's life was, was "just showing up." Jerry said he believed the rest was defined by hard work and luck.

Both of Jerry's children visited and it was when he and his daughter, then twenty-eight, hiked for miles to sit beneath a waterfall in Vietnam that she said, "Dad, you're really cool." Jerry asked her what she meant. "Well," she replied, "not many fathers would go to all this trouble."

Jerry said, "But I'm having a good time!"

"I know," said his daughter, "—that's what makes you cool."

It was, he said, the crowning moment of Jerry Gump's life.

Author's Mea Culpa

Lest anyone think I exploit my friends on these pages I want it known that except for those who are in jail or dead (two of whom died during the writing of the book), all were shown the text of their profiles and asked to sign off on the accuracy. This was done at the request of my publisher and, because I didn't want to lose any pals in the process, I went along.

I do not believe that the profiles suffered from the small deletions and alterations that were requested; only a few face-saving anecdotes were lost. The truth is, some of the subjects came back after reading the submitted draft with newer, more outrageous stories than they'd revealed during the years that we'd known each other and in interviews conducted for the book.

These people actually wanted to tell their stories, not as an act of braggadocio—although ego was never far away—but because they believed their discovery of self said something not only about themselves but also about their new homeland and what it meant to be an expatriate. They said it was in Thailand where they, in large and small ways, found or reinvented themselves, while, much to their delight, they encountered a contentedness they missed in earlier, less hospitable climes and domiciles.

Not long ago, I met a twenty-something French photographer, a recent arrival in Bangkok who said he was determined to stay. When I told him about some of the expats I was then proposing to include in this book, he asked if I thought his generation would make a similarly indelible mark. I said I didn't know. Perhaps the "dinosaurs"—a word used by several of the subjects here profiled— are or were just that, outsized creatures from another time, whose heirs and successors will be lizards and, at the largest, crocodiles. No slur intended, of course. But this book may be a celebration of a part of Southeast Asia that is sliding into the past, along with clean air and the *klongs* and many of the ancient mores and practices. That was then and this is now, as some wise man once said. Life goes on, bumpity-bump.

This is a book that celebrates bumpy Bangkok and the concept of escape. My dictionary has twelve meanings next to the word "escape." The first one says "to get away, as from confinement." That does it for me and, I think, everyone else in this book.